人 形
Dolls

多田敏捷

うつし絵
Transfer Seals

着せかえ
Dress-Up
Paper Dolls

ぬり絵
Coloring
Books

紫紅社文庫

Dolls: From the Edo Period to the Present-days

Gosho dolls

Gosho dolls were presentational dolls of little boys, first made in Kyoto during the early 18th century. The dolls were called by many names, and it was from the Meiji Period (1868–1912) on that they came to be widely known as *Gosho* (palace) dolls. The name comes from the Edo Period (1603–1867) system of *Sankin-kotai* (alternative attendance), which required feudal lords from western Japan to visit Edo (now Tokyo) every other year, their families kept there as permanent hostages to ensure loyalty to the Shogunate. On their way to Edo, it was customary for the lords to visit the Imperial Court and pay tribute, the *Gosho* doll being the return gift for their pains. Plate No. 1, the doll pulling a tortoise, was probably a gift sent by the Imperial Court on the occasion of the 11th Shogun Ienari's birth. The gift represented a wish for a strong and healthy boy and was most appropriate for a future warrior leader.

Karakuri dolls and *Ito-ayatsuri* dolls

Karakuri, or trick dolls, make use of elaborate pressure systems involving springs, mercury, water, sand, air and wind, or are operated with strings to give the illusion of movement. In the Heian Period work *Tales of Past and Present* (early 12th century), a water-operated *Karakuri* doll is reported to have protected a drought-infested rice paddy, but the dolls did not attract wide notice until the Edo Period when they were used in puppet plays in Takeda. *Ito-ayatsuri* dolls (marionettes) were first used in the late 1600's in plays by the Kyoto-based Yamamoto Kakudayu troupe, subsequently experiencing repeated cycles of decline and revival up to the present-day. When the Yuigi Magozaburo troupe continues to transmit the ancient skill of operating these dolls. Starting in the Meiji Period, marionettes were imported from Europe, and it is these Western-style marionettes which are commonly seen in children's puppet plays today.

Girls' Day dolls and accessories

The *hina* dolls used on Girls' Day (*hina matsuri*) have been in existence for centuries. The Heian Period classic *The Tale of Genji* (early 11th century) mentioned that "one and all are absorbed in play with *hina* dolls." The dolls were popularized in the Edo Period and *hina* play evolved into the *hina* festival (Girls' Day), the date of which became set at March 3. The dolls and accessories for the festival became more and more elaborate, the modern version consisting of a 5 to 7-tier stand and part or all of a set of 15 dolls, including the Emperor, Empress and other personages as well as various tiny accessories. As a set of dolls is extremely expensive and setting up the display is tremendously time-consuming, inexpensive and easy to play with "*hina* play" *omocha-e* (picture sheets) became quite popular with children.

Bunka dolls

Bunka ("culture") dolls were cloth dolls with modern Western clothing first introduced in the Taisho period (1912–1926). The true doll of the common people, they were very inexpensive, and are sure to be remembered fondly by any Japanese woman born before 1955. The dolls had dangling arms and legs and came in two types: one with a cloth face and drawn on eyes and nose which cried when its stomach was pressed, and the other with realistic three-dimensional facial features which said "Mama" when turned over.

Hug-me dolls

A naked doll in the form of a child, popular with young girls ages 5–6. The family would sew a *kimono* at home with which to clothe the doll.

Braid dolls

Dolls made of braid formed into the shapes of humans, animals and flowers. Supplies of braid to make one's own doll were sold along with finished dolls at fairs and cheap sweets shops.

Japanese paper dolls, cotton dolls and sew-on hair dolls

Dolls made of Japanese paper were frequently made in the shapes of animals. Cotton dolls were soft and wore out quickly, the result being that few remain in existence. Another doll could be made into various animals by sewing on "hair" made of silk thread. This was quite a high-grade toy, and few large examples can be found.

Wood-paste dolls

These dolls were made by kneading a sawdust-paste mixture until hard, then placing it in a mold, drying and coloring it. The finished product was lighter than clay and extremely durable. Plates No. 85–86 show examples of Osaka wood-paste dolls, which were popular from the late Meiji to the Taisho Period.

Milk-drinking doll

This doll came with a small milk bottle, which, when filled with water and brought to the doll's lips, caused the doll to drink the water. Originally an American doll, it was first produced domestically in 1954 and enjoyed great popularity for nearly a decade.

Curl doll

First marketed in 1957, this was a soft plastic doll with hair made of synthetic fibres which could be curled and styled. The doll could be washed in soap and water and its hair curled at fairly low temperatures (80–90 °C), making it a favorite with young girls.

Yajirobei (balancing toy)

A favorite with children from the Edo Period, when *Yajirobei* were depicted in *ukiyo-e* and picture books, to today, *Yajirobei* is a doll pierced with a rod laden with weights on either side. The weights regulate the doll's balance and keep it from falling over. Plate

No. 5 (commentary) and No. 104 (main text) show *Yashirobei* made from *Kamo* dolls of a fox and a child. These particular dolls, probably made for adults to be used at banquets and drinking parties, were made from high-quality materials and were no doubt very costly.

Transfer seals, Dress-up Dolls & Coloring Books

Transfer seals

Transfer seals have reversed images and patterns printed on a sheet of thin paper with water-soluble glue. The moistened seal is placed onto the skin and rubbed gently, then the backing is peeled off slowly so that the images are transferred to the skin as if they were tattoos. Originally this technique was invented for the decoration of pottery, metal and glass works; it was first used for children's toys during the late Meiji Period. Though it sounds very easy to transfer an image, one has to be careful when peeling the backing paper off in order to obtain a perfect image. Transfer seals were very popular during the Taisho and early Showa Periods; however, during the mid-1970s they disappeared from the market because licking the seals to moisten them was considered insanitary.

Dress-up paper dolls

One of the most typical of the games for girls is dress-up dolls. According to the *History of Japanese Dolls* edited by Tokubei Yamada in 1942, the first Japanese dress-up dolls were made during the early Edo Period (16th century) and called *hadaka ningyo* or "naked doll." They were made to be dressed in homemade costumes. Next, dolls called *ichimatsu-ningyo* with decorative, traditional costumes appeared. They could be undressed and redressed easily in a variety of costumes. However, for ordinary children, these dolls were too expensive. These children played with *anesama-ningyo* (literally:

elder sister doll) or three-dimensional female paper dolls made of *chiyogami* (figured paper) and colored paper. Nevertheless, to make *anesama-ningyo* required a degree of technique which was too difficult for young children. Therefore, "paper dress-up dolls" were created. They were made from woodblock printed paper on which human figures were depicted along with an assortment of dresses, hair styles, footwear and accessories. These images were intended to be cut out and assembled together. With woodblock prints, any kind of doll, luxurious costume or household utensil was within the attainable price range of any child. Moreover, they were easy to play with: children only had to cut out the pictures and assemble them. For these reasons they became very popular.

Paper dress-up dolls first appeared in the late Edo period (mid-19th century) and spread throughout the country along with *omocha-e* (children's picture sheets printed from woodblocks), which had dress-up dolls as one of their design themes. During the early Meiji Period, the Ministry of Education issued several versions of paper dress-up dolls with designs of Western costumes (No. 22, 23) to encourage Western dress and manners. Throughout the Taisho Period to the 1950s, paper dress-up dolls were the most typical toys for girls and, along with other toys, their designs vividly reflected the fashions and social conditions of the times. However, they became obsolete with the spread of television and three-dimensional dolls such as Barbie Dolls and Rika-chan Dolls. Now these two-dimensional dress-up dolls can only be found in some sweet shops or in a corner of the occasional small stationary shops. I hope that these lovely, inexpensive paper dress-up dolls will become popular again in the future.

Pictures to be colored and coloring books (*Nuri-e*)

Nuri-e (coloring picture game) used to be a popular pastime for children. *Nuri-e* sheets (picture sheet on which outlines of various figures were printed) first appeared during the early Meiji Period. They were used in elementary schools during the Meiji and Taisho Periods as an aid in art education. Towards the end of the Meiji Period, there was a boom in postcard coloring contests and many children took up the challenge of creating their own unique masterpieces by coloring in line drawings printed on postcards (No. 52). These contests accelerated the diffusion of picture sheets throughout the country. When *nuri-e* in book form (coloring books) were produced during the Taisho Period, they become one of the most popular pastimes for girls. However, as with other toys, because of the pervasive influence of television on our culture, coloring books have begun to gradually disappear from the market.

Kiichi's Coloring Books

Among the various toys made from the Meiji Period to the present, as far as I know the only one whose designer's name became familiar to all children and which was used for the product's name were "Kiichi's Coloring Books" (No. 71–97). Kiichi Tsutaya, born in Tokyo in 1914, was at first a painter of *nihonga* or Japanese style painting. After the Second World War, he started to design coloring books and began to publish them himself in 1947. His designs of fairyland princesses and animals captured the imagination of young girls and seemed to reflect their dreams in the era when peace was returning. His works began to be published by two *nuri-e* publishing houses and books with new designs were continuously produced. They were sold at every sweet shop throughout the country. Girls excitedly rushed to buy the latest issue and collected them like treasures. At their peak, around 1950–51, one million books were sold every month. It is not an exaggeration to say that in those days in Japan almost every girl played with a "Kiichi's Coloring Book." They were "hidden best sellers," which have never been mentioned in any history of Japanese children's culture.

人 形

うつし絵・着せかえ・ぬり絵

人形 ―江戸から現代まで―

○ 御所人形

　江戸時代に京都で生まれた美術的な人形で、その名称はいろいろあったが、「御所人形」という名称で広く呼ばれるようになるのは明治以降である。また西国大名が参勤交代で上府のとき、京の禁裏などに挨拶として目録を贈る風習があり、その時返礼にこの人形が贈られたのがその名の起こりという。

　御所人形はまた勅使下向の際、大奥などの土産として京千代紙ともども贈られたので、江戸では「お土産人形」といい、禁裏よりの御下賜品にこの人形が贈られる例がよくあったので「拝領人形」とも呼ばれた。

　安政以後、大阪今橋の人形店、伊豆蔵屋喜兵衛の人形が大阪以西に数多く販売されたので、これらの地域の人々は「伊豆蔵人形」とも呼んだ。図版No.1の「亀曳人形」は、11代将軍家斉誕生時に、多分禁裏あたりから贈られたものであろう。将来武士の棟梁たる人にふさわしい力強い人形である。

○ からくり人形

　ゼンマイや水銀、水、砂、空気(風)などを動力に利用したり、

紐を引いたりして動かす仕掛けになっている人形。平安時代の『今昔物語』に水からくりの人形が日でりの田を守ったことが記されているが、からくりが一般的に人々の目にふれるようになるのは、江戸時代になって、竹田のからくり人形芝居からである。またこのからくり人形は、神社祭礼の「山車人形」（山車からくり）にも応用された。

○ 連理返り

江戸時代のからくりを説明した代表的な本に『機巧図彙』がある。寛政8年（1796）に細川半蔵頼直によって書かれ、機械玩具の解説書としては江戸時代一番の本である。この中には「茶運び人形」「五段返り」「連理返り」「竜門の滝」「鼓笛児童」「揺盃」「闘鶏」「魚釣り人形」「品玉人形」の9種類の

（左）
大勝利人形
明治28年（1875）
12.4 × 6 × 4.7 cm
日清戦争の戦捷記念に買ってもらった人形。
"Great Victory Doll" made in commemoration of the Sino-Japanese War

（右）
大勝利人形の箱の側面
大勝利人形の文字
Side view of box for the "Great Victory Doll"

からくりが記されており、その中の一つ「連理返り」は、階段状の台を、2体の人形が両肩にかけた引合棒と呼ぶ2本の棒でつながり、この棒の中の水銀の移動によって棒が直立し、この時、人形も一緒にもち上り、下の人形を越してもう一段下の段におり、続いて次の人形が同じように下の人形を飛び越えて下におりていく。この様な動作をくりかえしながら下段におりていくからくり人形で、この時の様子を著者細川半蔵は本の中で次の様に書いている。「次第次第に下の檀へ落ちて立つこと何檀有ってもかわることなし　是もまことに生るが如し」

○ 糸操り

寛文・延宝(1661〜81)の頃、京都の山本角太夫一座が糸操りを角太夫節に合わせて演じたのが始まりで、その後たびたび廃れたがそのつど再興され、現在は結城孫三郎一座によってその技術が伝えられている。

これに対し、明治以降西洋式の糸操り人形マリオネットが輸入され、現在でもあちこちで公演され子供たちを喜ばせている。

○ 雛遊びの調度と人形

「雛遊び」の歴史は古く、平安時代の『源氏物語』に、「もろともにひいなあそびし給ふ」と記されている。この雛遊びが江戸時代に入ると一般化して「雛祭り」に移行し、年中行事として3月3日に定着した。「雛祭り」という言葉がうまれたのは江戸中期頃で、この頃から雛や調度品が少しづつ増

11

加し、雛壇の数も宝暦、明和(1751〜72)に2、3段となり、安永の頃(1772〜81)には4、5段の物も現われ、江戸末期には7、8段の物も見られた。雛壇に飾る人形や調度品は、一般的な物以外は当時の最高級品、最新流行の品などを調度品として並べ、また日頃愛玩している人形なども雛壇に並べた。段飾りの御雛様は大変高価で並べるのも大変であるが、おもちゃ絵や紙製の「おひなさま遊び」は安くて簡単に遊べるので、子供たちに大変人気があった。

○ 武者飾りと鯉幟

　江戸時代の初期、5月の節句に飾り兜やその他の武具、幟、吹き貫などを屋外に並べる風習が生まれたのが「武者飾り」のルーツ。

　「鯉幟」は、5月の節句に武士が玄関前に武家飾りを並べ立てたのに対抗して、江戸中期以後、町人が武具代りに、立身出世の魚として知られる鯉を幟として立てたのがおこりである。

○ 指人形

　人形の頭や手に指を入れ、指先を動かし、さまざまな動作をさせる人形を「指人形」という。玩具の指人形の歴史は古く、元禄3年(1690)刊、『人倫訓蒙図彙』に登場し、その後も人々に親しまれ現代におよんでいる。

　「指人形」の頭や手は、木、土、張り子、練り物等でつくられ、体の部分は布などでつくる。最近ではキャラクター物の「指人形」がよくつくられる。

○ 首振り人形

　子供の頃、母親に手をひかれ、よく夜店に行ったものであるが、その時、夜店の輪なげや射的場でよくこの人形を見かけたものである。人形の首が振動でゆっくりと、こっくり、こっくり動く姿は実にのどかで、ユーモラスである。

○ 姉様人形

　婦人の髪形をまねて、紙で髷を作り、千代紙などで衣裳をつくり、着せた人形。一般庶民の子供たちのままごと遊びの人形として古くから親しまれた。江戸時代には女の子の遊びとして広く各家庭で遊ばれ、江戸時代末期からは商品としても売り出された。

○ 縫いぐるみ人形

　綿やパッキングを芯にして、外側から布を縫い合わせて作った人形。
　江戸時代、家庭での手作りとして緋色の木綿の布で人形の形を作り、これに綿をつめ、これを「負い猿」と呼んだ。この「負い猿」を幼女たちは手に抱いたり、背負ったりした。これが縫いぐるみ人形の元祖である。

○ 文化人形

　大正時代に生まれた布製の抱き人形で、スタイルはモダンな洋装の人形だが、一番庶民的で安価な人形で、昭和30年以前に生まれた女性なら一番懐かしい人形がこの「文化人形」である。手足がぶらぶらしているので、「ぶらぶら人形」と

も呼ばれ、顔は布の上に目鼻を描いてあるのと、顔に凹凸があり、リアルに出来あがっているのと2種類ある。前者の方は腹部を押すと「キュー、キュー」と音のするのがあり、後者にはひっくりかえすと「マ、マー」と音のするのがあり、それは「ママー人形」とも呼ばれた。

○ 抱き人形
　童形の裸のままの日本人形で、5、6歳ぐらいの幼女の姿をしたものが多く、これに家庭で着物を縫って着せる。

○ モール人形
　モール細工で人形、花、動物などをこしらえたもの。縁日や駄菓子屋などで、材料のモールや出来がった人形などが売られた。

○ 土人形・石焼人形
　明治時代の子供のおもちゃ箱からよく土人形や石焼人形が出てくるが、いずれも手のひらの上に乗るような小型の物が多く、大きくても10センチ前後である。出てくる人形の種類は、天神、大黒、恵比須、稲荷のキツネ、子供の風俗人形等で、当時の子供に対する親の願い、子供の関心事がよくわかり大変おもしろい。

○ 和紙人形・綿人形・毛植人形
　「和紙人形」は和紙を材料にして製作され、作品は動物が多い。

「綿人形」は綿が材料のためやわらかく、すぐ潰れるため現存する作品が少ない。
　「毛植人形」は絹糸でできた毛を植えて、さまざまな動物が作られている。高級品のため大きな作品が少ない。

○ まくら人形・眠り人形・フランス人形
　「まくら人形」は縫いぐるみの抱き人形。枕の様な形をしているので「まくら人形」と呼ばれる。
　「眠り人形」は頭は陶製で、胴は練り物でできたものが多く、横に寝かせると人形のまぶたが下って眠った表情となる。
　「フランス人形」は昭和初期、フランスから人形の作り方が伝えられ、「フランス人形」の名で流行した。

○ 子供風俗人形
　その時代の代表的な子供衣裳を着たり、遊びをしている人形。

○ 練り物細工
　桐の鋸屑に糊を加えて練りかためたもの。またこれを型にいれて抜き、乾燥させ彩色すると土人形より軽く、堅牢なものが出来る。図版No. 72・73は、大阪練り物で明治末から大正時代にかけての物である。

○ ミルク飲み人形
　人形に付属しているミルク瓶に水を入れ、人形の口に当てがうと、その水を飲むのでこの名前がついた。元来はアメリ

カ生まれであったが、昭和29年(1954)に国産品がつくられるようになり、昭和30年代にかけて大流行した。

○ **カール人形**

　昭和32年(1957)から登場、合成繊維の髪をカールさせて髪結い遊びをする軟質ビニール製人形。値段は300円から800円ぐらい。セッケンで洗うことが出来、80〜90度ぐらいの高い温度で髪を好きな形に仕上げることが出来、少女たちにたいへん人気があった。

宣伝用ペコちゃん
昭和戦後 102 × 40 × 40 cm
Peko-chan (Fujiya Bakery's mascot doll)

やじろべえ・ペコちゃん
昭和戦後 16 × 16 cm
ソフトビニール製
Yajirobei with Peko-chan

○ バービー・スキッパー

　「バービー」は、昭和37年(1962)頃、アメリカから日本にはいってきた。39年頃から少学校高学年の少女を中心に全国的に大流行、衣裳も100種類ほどあり、髪型を変えるカツラまでそろっている。「バービー」の外に、妹の「スキッパー」、ボーイフレンドの「ケン」などのグループ人形もあり、着せかえ遊びの他に複雑な人形遊びも出来る。

　図版No. 77は、「バービー」の衣裳のサンプルとデザイン原画、型紙で、大変貴重なものである。

○ リカちゃん

　香山リカ、白樺学園5年生、5月3日生まれ、おうし座、血液型O型、音楽と体育が得意で算数が苦手(『リカちゃんとリカちゃんハウス』増渕宗一著より)。

　昭和42年(1967)に登場、それまでの外国感覚の人形から、純日本的人形(5等身、黒髪、べた足)に変わり、当時の少女たちに身近に感じられる人形として、たちまちのうちに少女たちの人気者となった。

○ GIジョー

　アメリカ兵の姿をした、男の子向きの着せかえ人形。人形の関節部分が21箇所も動き、本物の人間の様な動作が出来るのが特徴。兵士の種類も陸・海・空とあり、国別でもアメリカ、ドイツ、イギリス、フランスその他数ヵ国あり、付属兵器も数多く揃い、いろいろな組合わせが楽しめる。

　昭和39年(1964)アメリカでつくられ大流行。日本では昭和

41年から売り出され、男の子の兵隊着せかえ人形として人気者となった。

○ やじろべえ

　中心の人形から両横に棒をだし、その両端に重りを取り付け、左右の重さを平均させ、倒れないようにした玩具。享保の頃（1716〜36）には「張合人形」や「豆蔵」と呼ばれ、浮世絵や絵本に登場する。また「釣合人形」、「与次郎人形」、「弥次郎兵衛」、「笠人形」、「水汲人形」、「正直正兵衛」とも呼ばれ、江戸時代から現代まで子供たちに親しまれている。

　下の解説写真と本文図版No. 82の加茂人形の狐と童児のやじろべえは多分大人用で、酒席で用いられたものであろう。

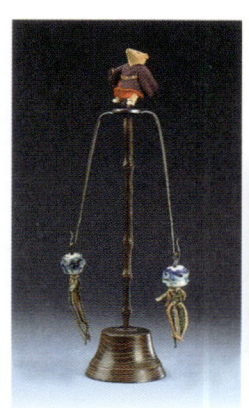

(左) やじろべえ・加茂人形
江戸時代 20 × 9 cm
Yajirobei (balancing toy) made from Kamo doll of a fox
(下) やじろべえ・ピエロ
1950s　11.5 × 18.5 cm　*Yajirobei* of Pierrot

この種類のやじろべえは加茂人形が多く、重りはギヤマンや玉が用いられ、やじろべえを支える主柱も唐木や金属、時にはギヤマンの棒も使用されることがある。当時としては非常に高価なものであったに違いない。

うつし絵・着せかえ・ぬり絵

○ うつし絵

　いろいろな絵を印刷した紙を水に濡らして、この絵を腕や手に貼り付けると、絵が紙から離れて皮膚に移る。この紙を「移し絵」という。

　明治の末期に陶磁器に模様を転写する技術を応用したものができた。台紙にのりを塗り、乾燥させてから、もう一度別ののりを塗り、その上から左右が逆になった絵を印刷する。台紙を水でぬらして、手の甲にあて、紙の裏からそっとこすり、ゆっくり紙をはがすと、絵が手の甲に移っている。一見簡単なように見えるが、はがし方にコツがあり、なかなかうまく出来ない。大正、昭和と子供たちの間で遊ばれたうつし絵も、昭和40年代にはいると、子供がなめるのは衛生上よくないと考えられ、しだいに子供たちの前から姿を消していった。

○ 着せかえ

　女の子の代表的な遊びに「着せかえ」がある。一般にいう「着せかえ遊び」とは、人物やいろいろな衣裳が印刷された一枚

の色刷りの紙から、人や衣服を抜きとり、衣裳の着せかえを楽しむ遊びをいうが、広い意味では、市松人形やバービー人形、リカちゃん人形などの衣裳の着せかえ、日本人形にいろいろなカツラをつけかえる遊びまで着せかえ遊びという。

　最近、紙の着せかえ遊びが少なくなったため、リカちゃん人形などの着せかえ遊びが主流になってきたが、本書では一番一般的に遊ばれた紙製の着せかえを見ていただきたい。

　着せかえ遊びのルーツは、人形にいろいろな衣裳を着せて遊んだのが最初であろう。昭和17年（1942）刊の『日本人形史』（山田徳兵衛）に「裸人形という言葉、その絵は西鶴の五人女に見える……、ふだんの玩び物として広く行われ、姉様や土人形にくらべると高級品であった。衣裳をも着せたであろう。」とあり、江戸時代の初期には広く裸人形で着せかえ遊びが行われていたことがわかる。また『日本人形史』には「裸

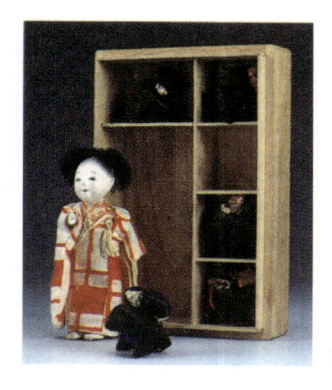

かつら替人形
13.5 × 9 × 3 cm
Doll with changeable wigs

人形に次いで、衣裳着の人形を子供がふだん玩ぶことが普通になった。衣裳を着せてあるのを買ったり、また家庭で縫って着せたりした。それを市松人形などと呼んだ」とあり、裸人形に次いで、市松人形の着せかえ遊びが、より広く家庭に普及していったことがわかる。しかし、いかに普及したとはいえ、市松人形などの着せかえ人形は、一般庶民、特に裏店の子供たちにとっては高根の花、姉様人形に、紙製の衣裳が精一杯であったであろう。しかし姉様人形といえども、姉様の製作には技術が必要であり、小さな子供たちには製作が困難である。そこで考えだされたのが、紙製の着せかえであろう。まず一枚の紙に木版で刷るので、人形とくらべると非常に値段が安く、一枚の紙から人や衣裳を切りとるだけですむので、姉様をつくったり、衣裳をつくったりする技術も手間もかからず、その上、木版で刷るため、どんな人形でも、ど

かつら替人形
19 × 12.5 × 4.4 cm
Doll with changeable wigs

21

んな立派な衣裳や調度品でも思うままである。これらのことが、紙製の着せかえが着せかえの主流になった原因であろう。

　紙製の着せかえは江戸後期頃から現われ、明治時代初期には文部省製本所発行の西洋着せ替などもつくられ、また、おもちゃ絵の普及にともない、木版刷りの安価な着せかえが一般に広まった。大正、昭和と、紙製の着せかえは、時代、世相を反映した図柄が印刷され、多くの幼女たちに愛用された。しかしテレビの普及や、バービー、リカちゃんなどの人形の流行により紙製着せかえは廃れ、現在では駄菓子屋や、文具店の片隅でほそぼそと売られている状態である。安価な紙製着せかえが再び日の目を見る日を期待したい。

○ ぬり絵

　画用紙などの紙面に、いろいろな絵の輪郭だけが描かれていて、この絵の輪郭にそって色を塗っていく絵紙を「ぬり絵」

かつら替人形
13.5 × 8.7 × 3 cm
Doll with changeable wigs

という。
　一枚ものから数枚をとじ合せたぬり絵帳まであり、女の子の遊びとしては大変人気があった。
　江戸時代の木版刷の本の中に、色のない挿絵に、いたずらがきで輪郭にそって彩色をしたものを時々みかけることがある。この中には大人がしたのではないかと考えられる上手なものから、明らかに子供と考えられる稚拙なものまでいろいろあるが、大部分、子供のいたずらと考えられるものが多い。本物のぬり絵ではないが、輪郭にそって色を塗った点ではぬり絵遊びのルーツともいってもよいのではないか。明治時代になると、学校教育として図画の絵手本に色を塗ることが行われ、明治後期には、ハガキに絵が描かれていて、それに色を塗って送ると、賞金や賞品がもらえることが流行し、多くの子供たちがこれに挑戦し、このことがぬり絵の流行に拍車

かつら替人形
18.5 × 12 × 3.5 cm
Doll with changeable wigs

をかけた。大正時代になるとぬり絵帳も現れ、以後ぬり絵は、女の子の遊びの代表的なものになった。

○ きいちのぬり絵

明治時代から現代まで、子供たちに親しまれた玩具は色々あるが、作者の名前が玩具の呼び名と共に呼ばれ、多くの子供たちに親しまれたのは、筆者の知るかぎり、「きいちのぬり絵」ぐらいであろう。

昭和20年代の初め、日本の子供たちにやっと平和が訪れた頃、日本のあちこちの露地裏の駄菓子屋で、次々と売りだされるきいちのぬり絵に、女の子たちは目を輝かし、先を争っ

て買い求め、宝物のごとく慈しんだものである。

　昭和25、6年頃には全国で月100万枚前後も売られ、当時の女の子たちは、みんなきいちのぬり絵で遊んだと言っても過言ではない。児童文化史の表面には現われない、隠れたベストセラーである。

　現在、日日にきいちのぬり絵が、いやぬり絵文化そのものが忘れられていくのが非常に残念である。紙に描かれたおとぎ話の主人公に、動物たちに、子供たちの夢をぬりかさねていくぬり絵も、たまには良いのではなかろうか。

○ 蔦谷喜一 伝

　大正3年(1914)2月18日、東京の京橋の紙問屋「蔦谷商店」の子として生まれる。家業が新聞用紙を扱う商店だったため、商業高校に入れられるが、商業算数や簿記は苦手で、子供の頃から人物を描くのが好きであったので、4年目に学校を中退、昭和7年(1932)に川端画学校へ入学、本格的に日本画を勉強する。

　昭和14年(1939)、画学校時代の友人にすすめられ、アルバイトで「汐汲」や「藤娘」など数種類の歌舞伎踊りのぬり絵を描く。当時、夏目漱石の「虞美人草」の藤尾に憧れていたので、ぬり絵に「フジヲ」という名前を入れた。

　昭和17年(1942)、物資統制でぬり絵屋が廃業、その後海軍に徴用される。

　昭和20年(1945)8月、終戦で家に帰り、友人の紹介で、進駐軍の軍人や家族の肖像画を描く。一年程すると、以前描いていたぬり絵屋さんがたずねてきたのでぬり絵を再開、しか

し、3、4ヵ月でやめ、22年1月から、「キイチ」の名前で、おとぎの国のお姫様などを描いたぬり絵を自費出版する。しかし製作と販売の二役はむずかしく、結局、22年夏頃から、喜一、石川、川村の三者の共同経営で出発、昭和23年には、川村さんの山海堂と石川さんの石川松戸堂の二軒にわかれ、二軒からきいちのぬり絵が出版された。

　昭和25、6年がきいちのぬり絵のピークで、100万枚前後も売れたという。

　二羽の小鳥が、短冊の両端をくわえているのが石川松戸堂で、アルファベットのTの下にサインが入り、Tの字に小鳥が一羽止まっているのが、山海堂である。

　昭和37、8年頃から、テレビの普及などで、ぬり絵の需要も減り、45、6年頃には、きいちのぬり絵は、子供世界から消えてしまった。しかし、最近きいちのぬり絵が、再びよみがえり、ところどころで、その姿を見かけるようになった。玩具を愛するものとしては、大変喜ばしいことである。

[参考文献]
- 『日本人形史』山田徳兵衛著　冨山房　昭和17年(1942)
- 『東京玩具人形問屋協同組合70年史』70周年記念事業委員会編　東京玩具人形問屋協同組合　昭和31年(1956)
- 『日本人形玩具辞典』斎藤良輔編　東京堂出版　昭和43年(1968)
- 『おもちゃの話』斎藤良輔著　朝日新聞社　昭和46年(1971)
- 『日本のおもちゃ』山田徳兵衛著　芳賀書店　昭和46年(1971)

- 『日本のおもちゃ遊び』斎藤良輔著　朝日新聞社　昭和47年(1972)
- 『日本こども遊び集』(太陽No. 140) 平凡社　昭和49年(1974)
- 『日本の人形と玩具』西沢笛畝著　岩崎美術社　昭和50年(1975)
- 『子どもの四季』三井良尚著　時事通信社　昭和51年(1976)
- 『浮世絵の見方』吉田漱著　渓水社　昭和52年(1977)
- 『昭和玩具文化史』斎藤良輔著　住宅新報社　昭和53年(1978)
- 『きいちのぬりえ』蔦谷喜一著　草思社　昭和53年(1978)
- "Barbie Dolls" Paris, Susan & Carol Collector Books 1982
- 『玩具の今昔』(特別展図録) 市立市川歴史博物館　昭和59年(1984)
- 『青い眼の人形』武田英子著　山口書店　昭和60年(1985)
- 『明治・大正・昭和　子ども遊び集』(別冊太陽) 平凡社　昭和60年(1985)
- 『おもちゃの歴史と子どもたち』(特別展図録) 小山市立博物館　昭和60年(1985)
- 『夢をつむぐ』尾崎秀樹著　光村図書出版　昭和61年(1986)
- 『浮世絵の基礎知識』吉田漱著　雄山閣　昭和62年(1987)
- 『テーマは遊』(特別展図録) 兵庫県立歴史博物館　昭和63年(1988)
- 『遊びとおもちゃ』(特別展図録) 埼玉県立博物館　昭和63年(1988)
- 『リカちゃんハウスの博覧会』増渕宗一監　INAX　平成元年(1989)
- 『おもちゃ博物誌』斎藤良輔著　騒人社　平成元年(1989)
- 『おもちゃの歴史』(特別展図録) 大分市歴史資料館　平成元年(1989)
- "Collectible Male Action Figures" Paris & Susan Collector Books 1990
- 『よし藤・子ども浮世絵』中村光夫著　富士出版　平成2年(1990)
- 『遊びとおもちゃ』(特別展図録) 栃木県立博物館　平成3年(1991)
- 『懐かしのおもちゃ展』(特別展図録) 市立函館博物館　平成3年(1991)

● 著者――多田敏捷（ただ としかつ）
- 昭和16年7月7日生まれ
- 著者の玩具コレクションは平成21年1月16日に大阪府の有形民俗文化財に多田コレクションとして指定される
  http://www.pref.osaka.lg.jp/bunkazaihogo/bunkazai/yuukei.html
- コレクションは大阪府が買い上げ、現在は国立民族博物館が所蔵している
- 国公立博物館評価鑑定の第一人者として現在も精力的に活動している

《主な実績》
- 兵庫県立歴史博物館　入江コレクションの評価鑑定
- 鳥取わらべ館では資料館設立に参画
- 白い恋人パーク博物館が東京のアンティークショップ老舗「パニポート」のコレクションを買い上げる際の鑑定、また同館のブリキのおもちゃの解説、評価鑑定も行っている

＊本書は、平成9年4月発行の「京都書院アーツコレクション」―『人形 DOLLS』を改訂・新装本としたものです。

協力：ぬりえ美術館 館長 金子マサ

DOLLS

Transfer Seals, Dress-up Paper Dolls & Coloring Book

御所人形
Gosho Doll

1 御所人形・亀曳人形
   (左) 蓬莱亀
   34.2 × 21 × 22.5 cm
   (右) 人形
   40 × 28 × 18 cm
   11代将軍家斉誕生の時
   贈られた人形。
   Gosho doll:
   Boy pulling a tortoise

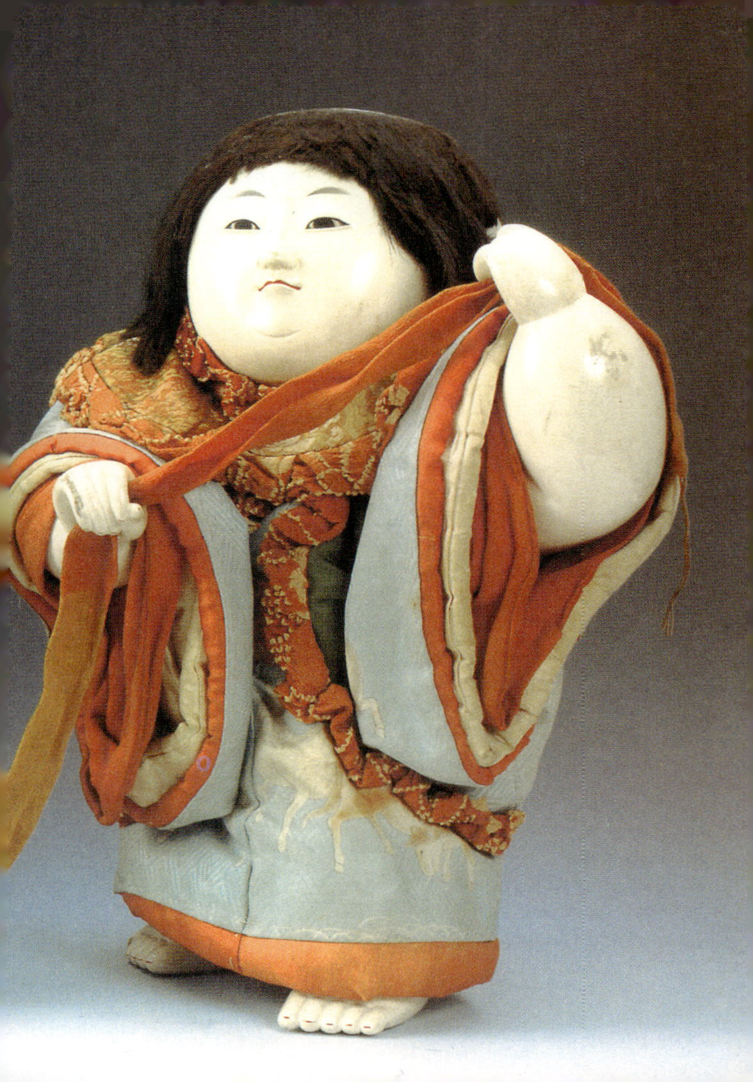

からくり人形
Karakuri Doll

2 連理返りの箱
江戸後期　19.5 × 10 × 13 cm
Box for a *Karakuri*-doll (trick doll) set

箱を開くと中に連理返りの人形が収納され、箱が階段になる。
Disassembled set

33

引合棒が水銀の移動によって直立したところ。
Dolls standing upright operated by mercury

一段下におりたところ。
Dolls coming down the stairs

連理返りの人形を置いたところ。
Assembled set

3 少女と犬
1900s　15 × 12 × 9.5 cm
ゼンマイ動力で少女の手と犬の前足が動く。
Karakuri doll: the girl's arms and the dog's front paw move by clockwork

4　輪を持つ少女
1890s　16.5 × 5.5 × 5.5 cm
下の台に針金とふいごが仕掛けてあり、下方に押すと音がし、針金が上に突き上げられ人形の内部のからくりを動かし、輪を持った手が上にあがる。
Karakuri doll: a wire and bellows cause the girl's arms, holding a hoop to move up

5　小鳥と花
1900s　10 × 9 × 6 cm
下の台に針金とふいごが仕掛けてあり、下方に押すとピーピーと小鳥の鳴き声がし、針金に押されて小鳥が動く。
Karakuri doll: a wire and bellows cause the bird to sing and move

6　ネズミの輪まわり　1910s　10×9×6 cm
籠の下の台にふいごが仕掛けてあり、下方に押すと音がして台の上部より風が吹き出して、ネズミのまわりのセルロイド製の輪をまわし、まるでネズミ自身が動いて輪をまわしているように見える。
Karakuri doll: bellows cause a hoop to move around a mouse

7
首さげ人形
1910s　16.7 × 7 × 3.5 cm
人形を首からぶらさげて歩くと、その振動で人形が上下し、また腹部に仕掛けられたふいごが鳴る。
Karakuri doll: when hanging from one's neck, the walking vibration causes the doll to move up and down

8　少女
1910s　17 × 6.5 × 4.5 cm
人形からのびたゴム管に接続したふいごを押すと少女の手が上にあがる。
Karakuri doll: bellows move the girl's arms up

操り人形　*Ayatsuri* Doll

9　糸操り人形　江戸時代後期　23 × 26.5 × 2 cm
Ito-ayatsuri doll（marionette）

三月人形
Hina Doll

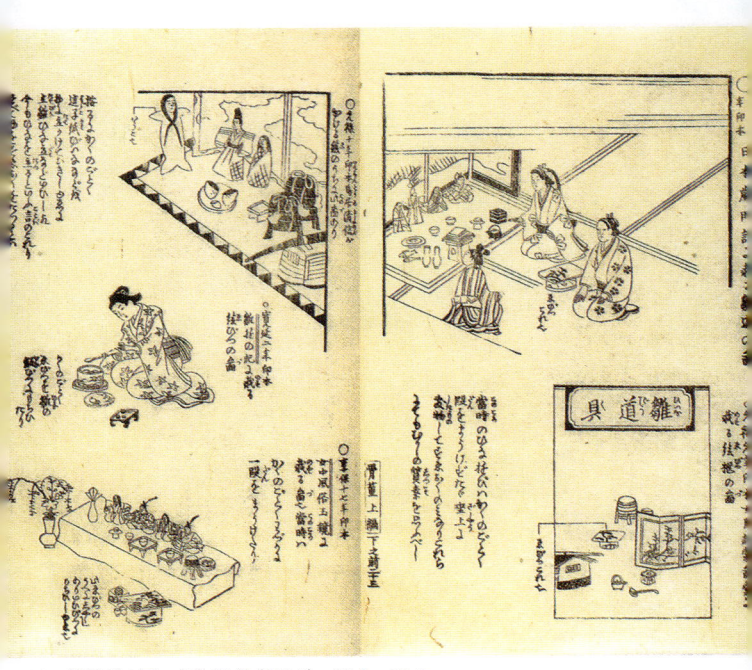

10 雛遊びの図　文化11年（1814）　26.5 × 18.5 cm
　『日本歳時記』にのる雛遊の図　『骨董集』（上編下の前）　山東京伝
　Illustrations of girls playing with *hina* dolls

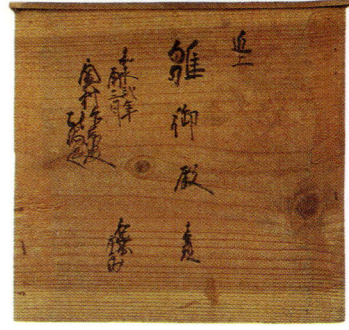

11 雛御殿
　　嘉永2年（1849）
　　28 × 27.5 × 22 cm
　　Place of *hina* dolls

雛御殿の箱蓋
Box lid for *hina* dolls

12　ギヤマンの雛道具
　　6 × 10.3 × 5.9 cm
　　高杯、鉢、ワイングラスが入る幕末の高級雛道具。
　　A set of glassware for *hina* dolls

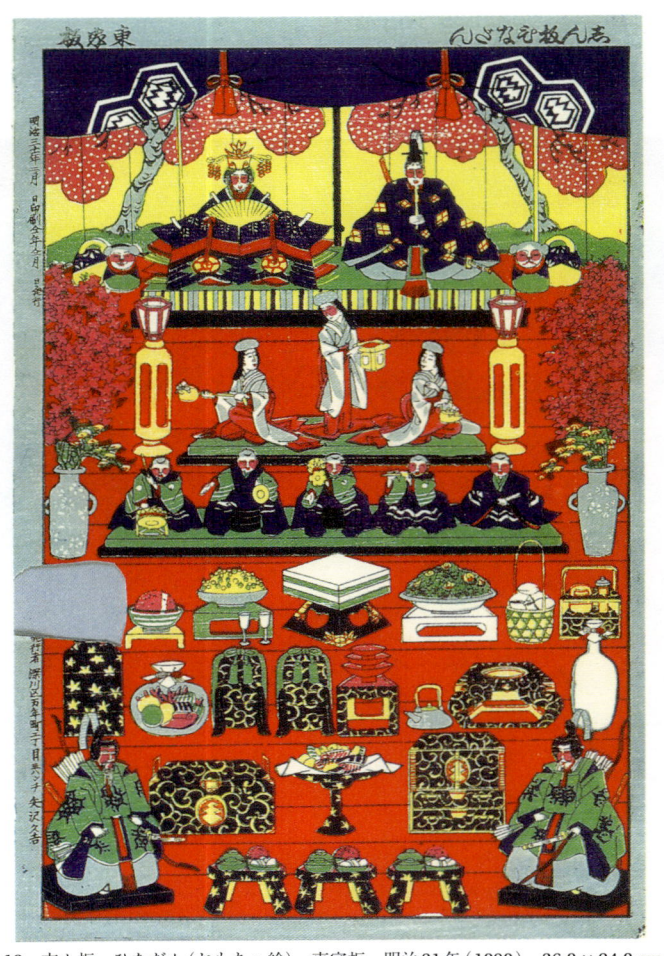

13　志ん板　ひ␣なだん（おもちゃ絵）　東家板　明治31年（1898）　36.8 × 24.8 cm
Omocha-e（picture sheet）of *hina* dolls

14 おひなさまあそび 1940s 38.5 × 27 cm
Picture sheet of *hina* dolls

15 おひなあそび 1950s 30 × 20.8 cm アサヒ玩具製
Picture sheet of *hina* dolls

五月人形 Boys' Day Decorations

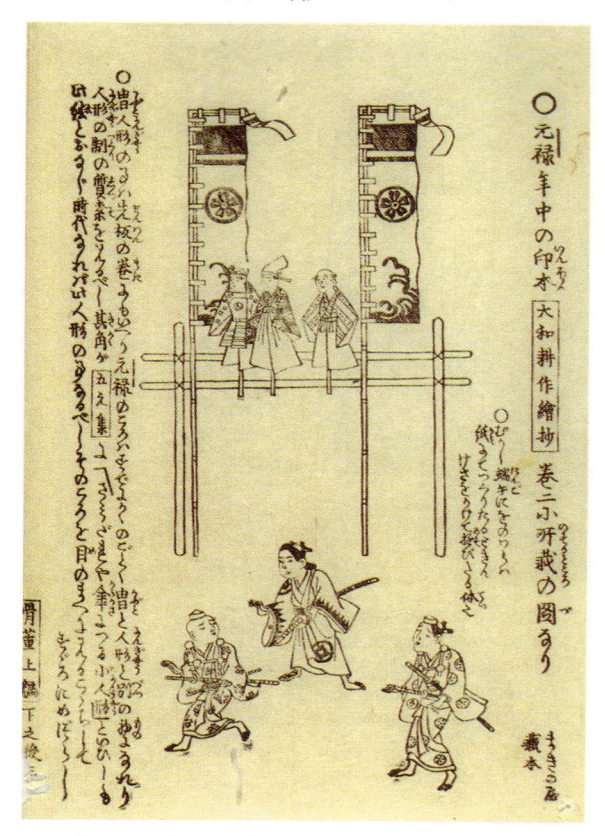

16　元禄年間の五月節供の外飾
　　文化11年（1814）　26.5×18.5 cm　『骨董集』（上編）　山東京伝
　　Boys' Day outdoor decorations used during the Genroku Era
　　（1688–1704）

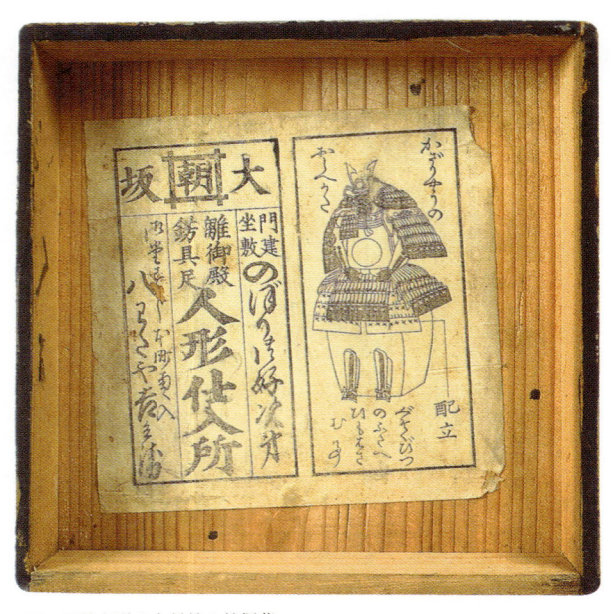

17　五月人形の大将鎧の鎧櫃蓋
1850 〜 68年　22 × 21.7 cm
内側に木版刷の鎧の飾り方と、宣伝文が書かれている。
人形仕入所・八幡屋吉兵衛
Lid of case for the armor

大将鎧 ▶
1850 〜 68年　53.5 × 23 × 23 cm
Boys' Day *samurai* armor

51

18　飾太鼓
1860s　11 × 42 × 11.5 cm
Boys' Day ornamental drum

Boys' Day *samurai* decorations and carp streamers

On the annual festival of May 5 (Boys' Day), a custom began in the early Edo Period of displaying helmets, arms, streamers, banners and other *samurai* accessories outside one's home. Carp streamers first appeared when Edo merchants, in opposition to the *samurai*'s elaborate outdoor displays of weapons, responded in turn by hoisting streamers in the form of carp, fish symbolizing advancement in life and career, outside their dwellings.

19 ざしきのぼり
安政2年(1855)
35.5 × 25.5 cm
芳綱画　辻岡屋版
Woodblock print with carp streamers

20　武者飾り　安政3年（1856）　25×36 cm　芳幾画
Woodblock print with Boys' Day decoration

55

21　鯉幟　安政2年（1855）　37.5 × 25.5 cm　芳藤画　文正堂
Woodblock print of carp streamers

57

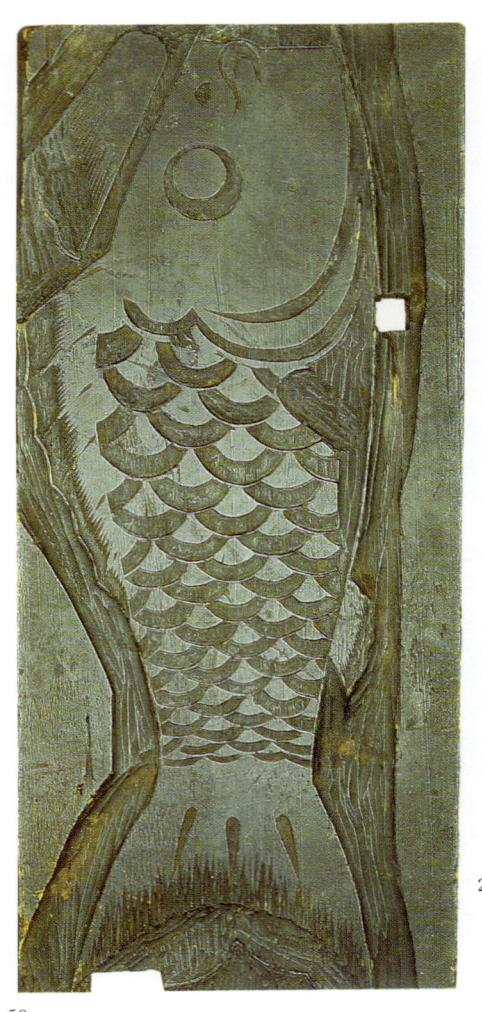

22　鯉幟の版木
　　幕末〜明治初期
　　46 × 20 cm
　　Woodblock for a
　　carp streamer

23　ノブヤの組立武者かざり　1950s　39 × 26.9 cm
Cut-out, fold-up picture sheet with Boys' Day decoration

指人形
Finger Puppets

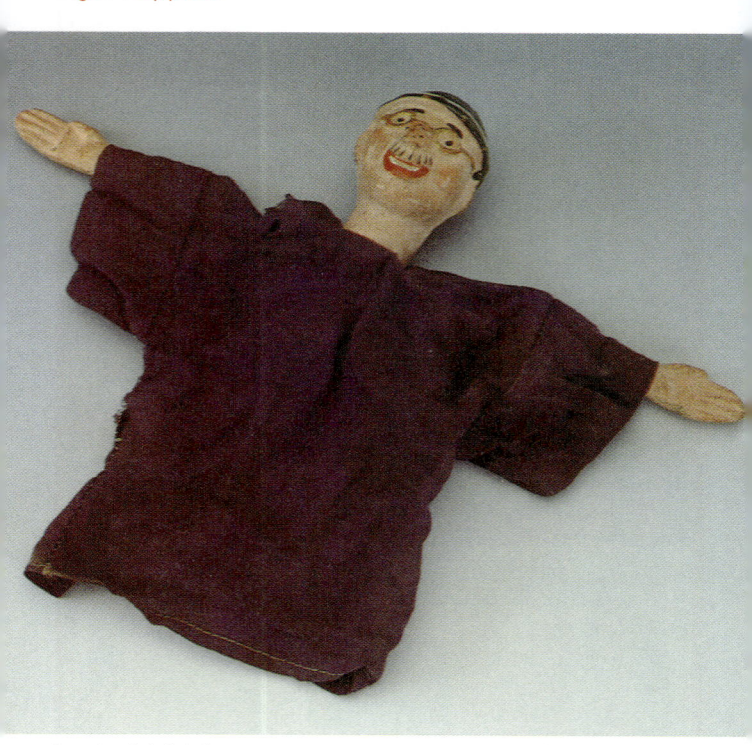

24　ノンキナトウサン　1920s　21 × 26 cm　Happy-go-lucky Father

25　指人形　(左)金五郎　(右)娘　1940s　20 × 22 cm　Finger puppets

Finger puppets

By inserting a finger into the arm or head area of the doll and bending the finger, a whole repertoire of actions are made possible. Finger puppets have a long history in Japan, appearing in the 1690 work *Compendium of Human Enlightenment*, and are still loved by children today. With cloth bodies and heads and hands made of wood, clay and papier-mache, modern finger puppets are often made in the forms of popular children's characters.

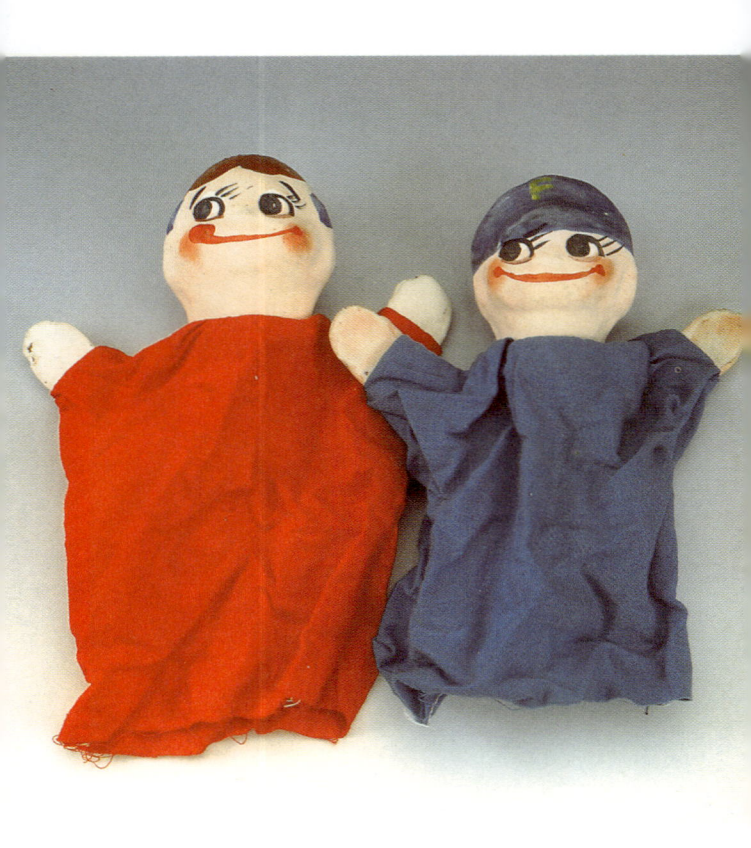

26 ペコちゃん ポコちゃん 1950s 20 × 17.5 cm
Peko-chan & Poko-chan

27　指人形　1960s　20×17 cm　Finger puppets

首振り人形　Neck-shaking Dolls

28　首振り人形　1920s　18.5 × 7 × 7 cm
Neck-shaking doll

29　首振り人形　レーサー　1950s　10.5 × 5.5 × 6 cm
Neck-shaking doll: Racer

30 首振り人形　（左）野球少年　（右）エンタツの桃太郎
1950s　10 × 5 × 4.5 cm
Neck-shaking dolls

エンタツの桃太郎の首を取ったところ
Disassembled doll

Kubifuri doll

In my childhood, I can remember being taken at night by my mother to open-air night stalls and fairs, and I recall *kubifuri* (head-shaking) dolls being omnipresent at the ring-toss stalls and shooting galleries. When moved, the dolls gently shake their heads in a nodding motion which is genuinely humorous.

姉様人形　*Anesama* Dolls

31　姉様を作る図　当世美人合　33.5 × 21 cm　国貞画　和泉屋板
Woodblock print of girl making *anesama* dolls

32 あねさま子供風俗　明治30年（1897）　35.3 × 23.5 cm　宮川春汀画
Woodblock print of girls playing with *anesama* dolls

33　姉様　明治時代　16 × 6 × 4 cm　*Anesama* doll

Anesama doll

These dolls imitate ladies' hairstyles and fashions, with the hair "styled" in paper chignons and clothes made of patterned paper (*chiyogami*). *Anesama* (elder sister) dolls, used in playing house, have been popular with the masses for centuries, being present in virtually every young girl's home in the Edo Period. They began to be produced and sold commercially in the final Edo years.

34　姉様のいろいろ　明治〜昭和　47 × 9 × 3.3 cm　Variations of *anesama* dolls

縫いぐるみ人形　Stuffed Dolls

35　犬　1890s　16.5 × 17 × 10 cm　Dog

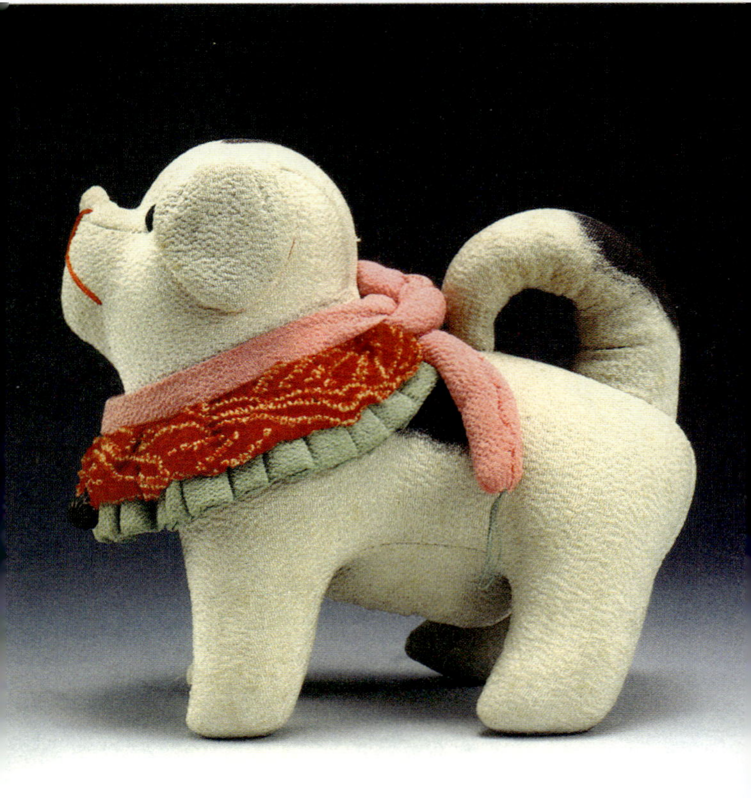

36　猫　1900s　17 × 10.5 × 10 cm　Cat

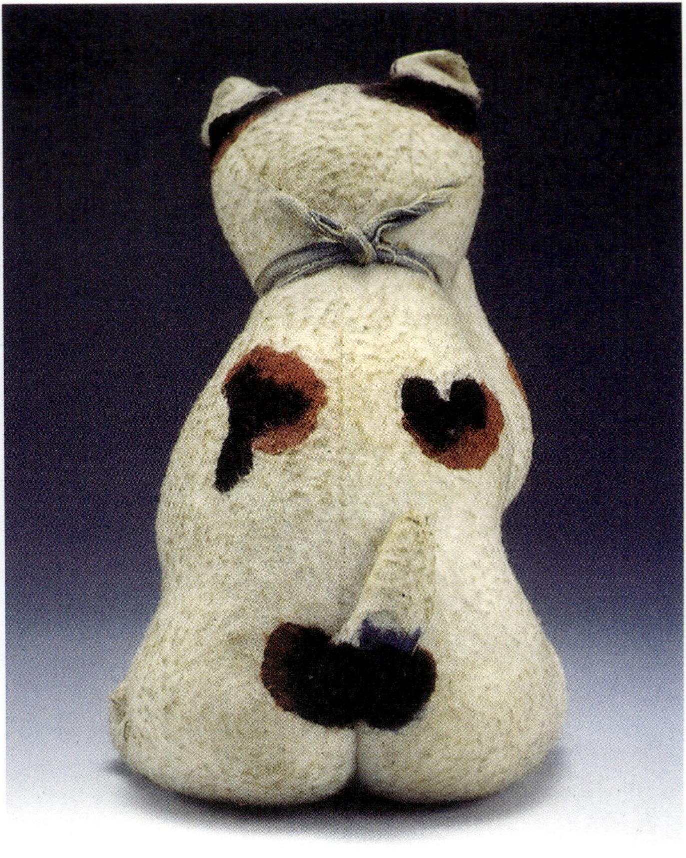

37　犬　1900s　12 × 17 × 7 cm　Dog

77

38 小犬
1910s 6.5 × 14 cm
Puppy

Stuffed dolls

Cloth dolls stuffed with cotton or packing have been popular in Japan since the Edo Period, when homemade monkey dolls with pink cotton bodies and cotton stuffing were played with by little girls. The dolls enjoyed great popularity and were the forerunners of other Japanese stuffed toys.

39　うさぎ　1900s　12.5 × 21 × 10.5 cm　Rabbit

40 うさぎ 1920s 17 × 9 × 18 cm Rabbit

41　犬　14 × 8.5 × 13 cm　Dog

42　犬　1930s　25.5 × 19 × 10 cm　Dogs

83

43 文化人形　大正〜昭和　20 × 57 × 34 cm　*Bunka* ("culture") dolls

文化人形
Bunka Dolls

44　文化人形　1920s　36 × 16 × 8.5 cm　ママ笛入り
Bunka ("culture") doll

45　文化人形　1926～60年　50×25×9.5 cm　*Bunka* dolls

46 文化人形
1926〜60年
41 × 17 × 5 cm
Bunka dolls

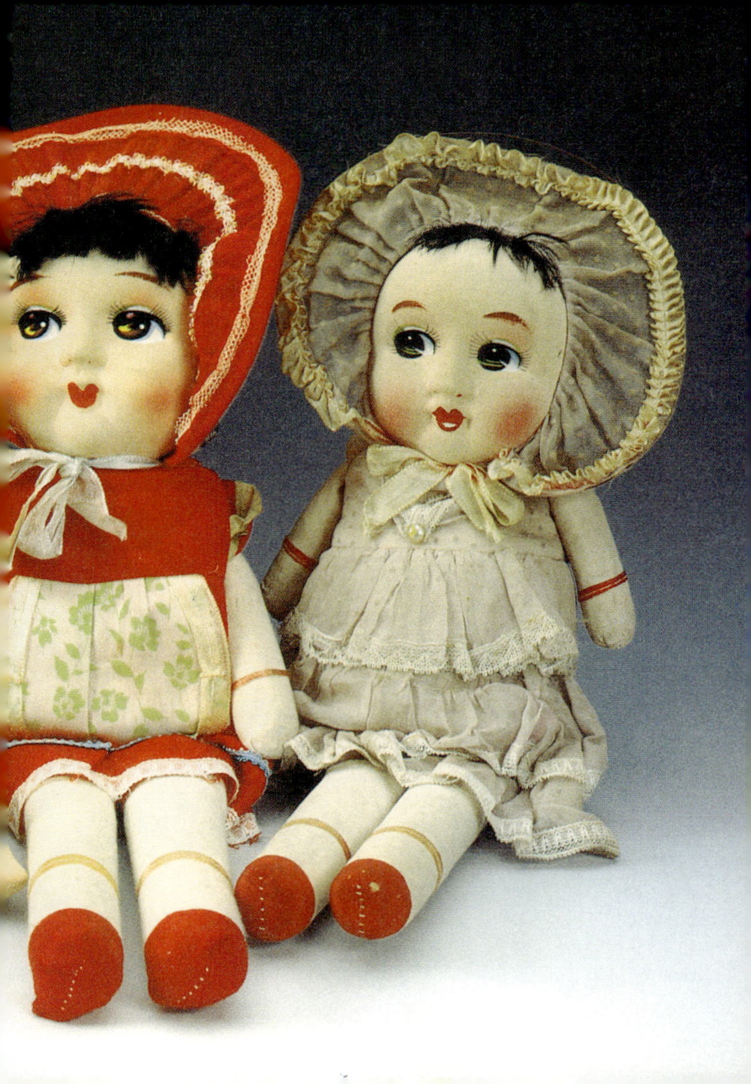

抱き人形 Hug-me Dolls

47
抱き人形
明治時代
19.5 × 9 × 9.5 cm
Hug-me dolls

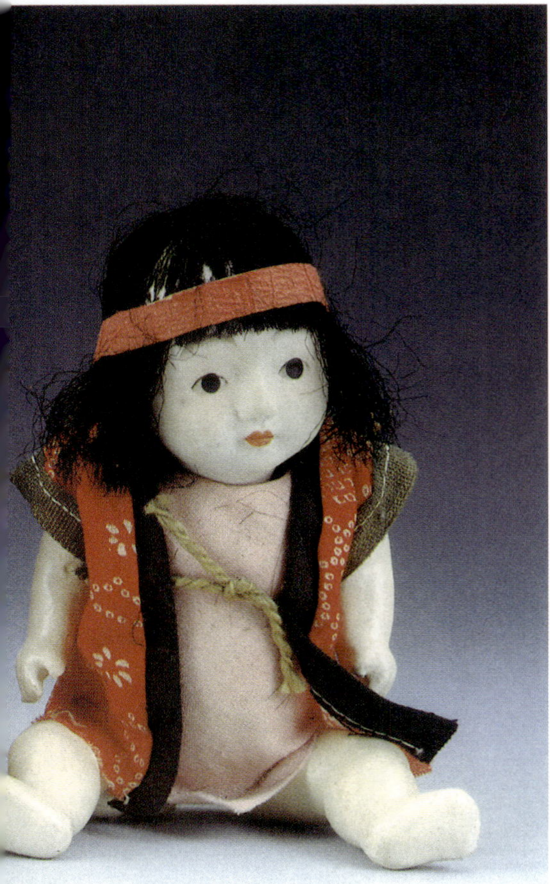

48　抱き人形　1920s　23 × 15 × 13 cm　Hug-me doll

49　抱き人形　1940s　41 × 9 × 9 cm　Hug-me doll

モール人形
Braid Dolls

モール細工の材料　Pieces of braid

50　モール細工の花　1930s　17 × 9 × 9 cm　Braid flowers

51　モール人形　1930s　10.5 × 7.3 cm　Braid dolls

52 モール人形 1950s 24 × 5 cm Braid dolls

53　モール人形　1950s　12 × 3.2 cm　Braid dolls

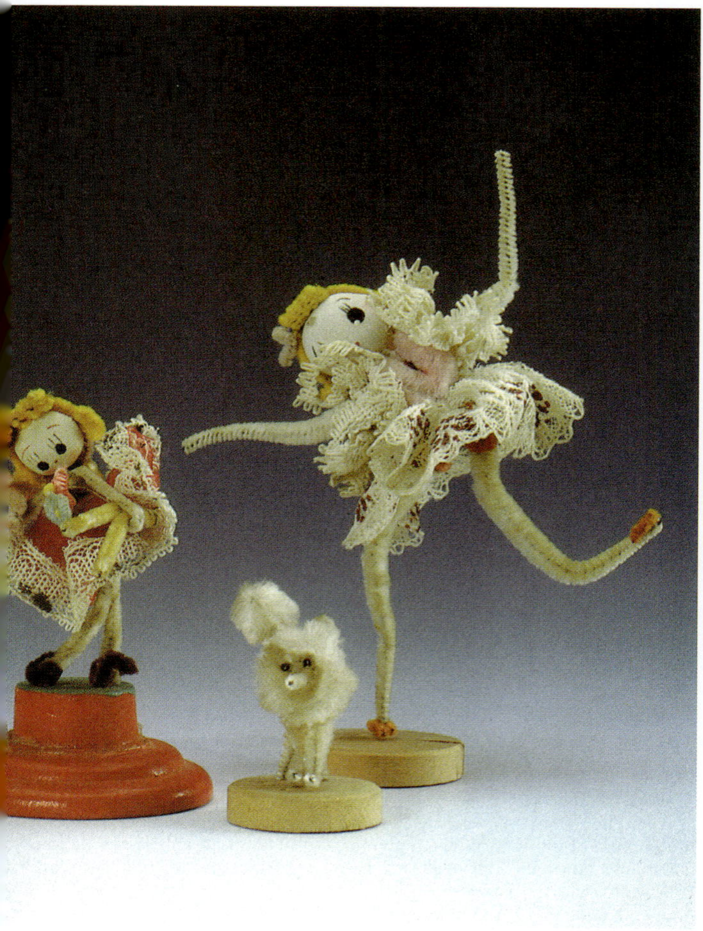

土人形
Clay Dolls

54 ラケットを持つ少年
明治末〜大正初期
12 × 9.8 × 5.5 cm
Clay doll: Boy
holding a racket

Cray and porcelain dolls

Clay and porcelain dolls, nearly all under 10 cm long and small enough to fit in the palm or one's hand, were popular in the Meiji Period. The dolls were commonly representations of gods of the heavens, luck and wealth, or the foxes believed to act as messengers for the agricultural god *Inari*. Still others illustrated popular trends and manners of the day, and are invaluable in showing as the interests of children of the period, as well as the beliefs of adults and what they wished for their children.

55 なわとび　明治末〜大正初期　7.5 × 5.5 × 4.5 cm
Clay doll: Girls with a jumping rope

56 恵比須様と天神様
明治時代　7 × 5.5 × 1.7 cm
Porcelain dolls: Ebisu god & Tenjin god

石焼人形
Porcelain Dolls

57 稲荷のキツネ
大正初期　5.8 × 4 × 2.3 cm
Porcelain dolls: Foxes of Inari Shrine

58 石焼人形　明治時代　9 × 3.8 × 2.5 cm
Porcelain dolls: Military man, girl with a doll, student (from left to right)

59 石焼人形　犬
明治時代
6 × 4 × 2.5 cm
Porcelain doll:
Dog

60 石焼人形　明治時代　4.5×3×2 cm　Porcelain dolls

61 石焼人形　大正時代　6.5×3×1.5 cm　Porcelain dolls

綿人形　Cotton Doll

62　綿人形　うさぎ　明治時代　11 × 4 × 4 cm　Cotton doll: Rabbit

和紙人形　Japanese Paper Dolls

63　和紙人形　猫　明治時代　9 × 9 × 4 cm　Japanese paper doll: Cat

64　和紙人形　うさぎ　明治時代　18 × 10 × 5.5 cm
Japanese paper doll: Rabbit

65　和紙人形　たぬき　大正時代　8 × 7 cm
Japanese paper doll: Racoon dog

毛植人形
Sew-on Hair Doll

66 毛植人形　狆
　江戸時代
　23 × 25 × 9 cm
　Sew- on Hair doll:
　Pug dog

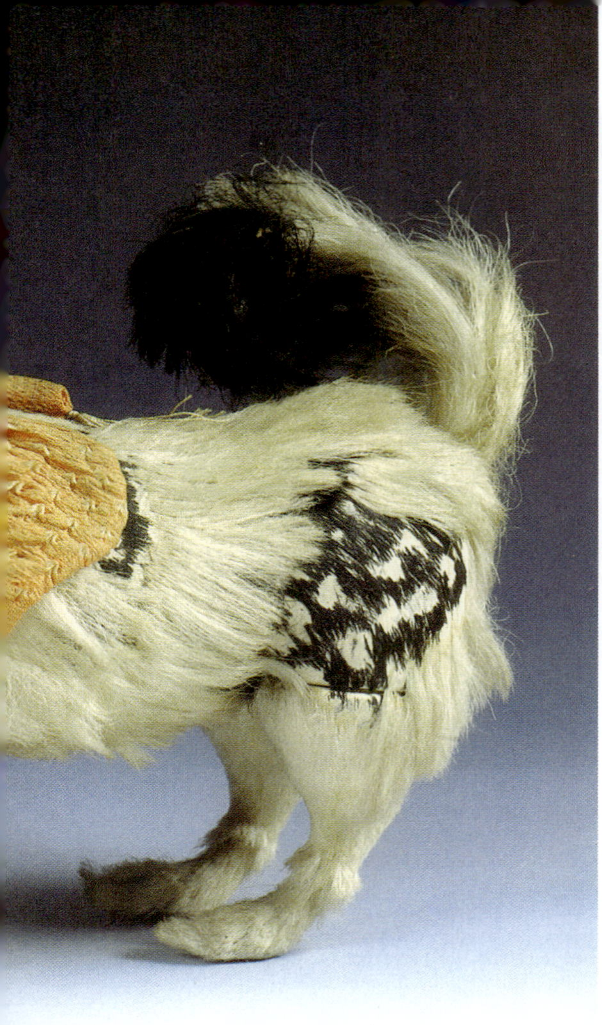

まくら人形　Pillow Dolls

67　まくら人形　1910s　35 × 14 × 9 cm　Pillow dolls

Pillow dolls, sleepy-head dolls, French dolls

Pillow dolls were stuffed toys in the general shape of pillows made to hugged by children. Sleepy-head dolls had ceramic heads and wood-paste torsos, and closed their eyes when laid down to convey the illusion of sleep. At the beginning of the Showa Period (1926–1989) the French way of dollmaking was introduced to Japan, and dolls produced in this manner, called French dolls, were considered quite stylish.

68 まくら人形　猫を抱いた少女　1920s　19 × 8 × 5 cm
Pillow doll: Girl holding a cat

眠り人形　Sleepy-Head Doll

69 眠りベビードール
　1940s　14 × 26 × 7 cm
　Sleepy- head doll
　腹部をおすと泣く。

フランス人形　French Doll

70　フランス人形　1930s　35 × 17 × 13 cm　French doll

子供風俗人形
Children's Popular Dolls

71 子供風俗人形
1900s
15 × 6 × 4.3 cm
Children's
popular dolls

Children's popular dolls

Dolls dressed in the typical clothing and engaged in the popular games of the day.

練り物細工　Wood-Paste Dolls

72　玉乗り　15 × 9 × 2 cm　大阪練り物
Wood-paste doll: Dancer on a ball

73 犬　12 × 9.5 × 4 cm　大阪練り物
Wood-paste doll: Dog

ミルク飲み人形
Milk-Drinking Doll

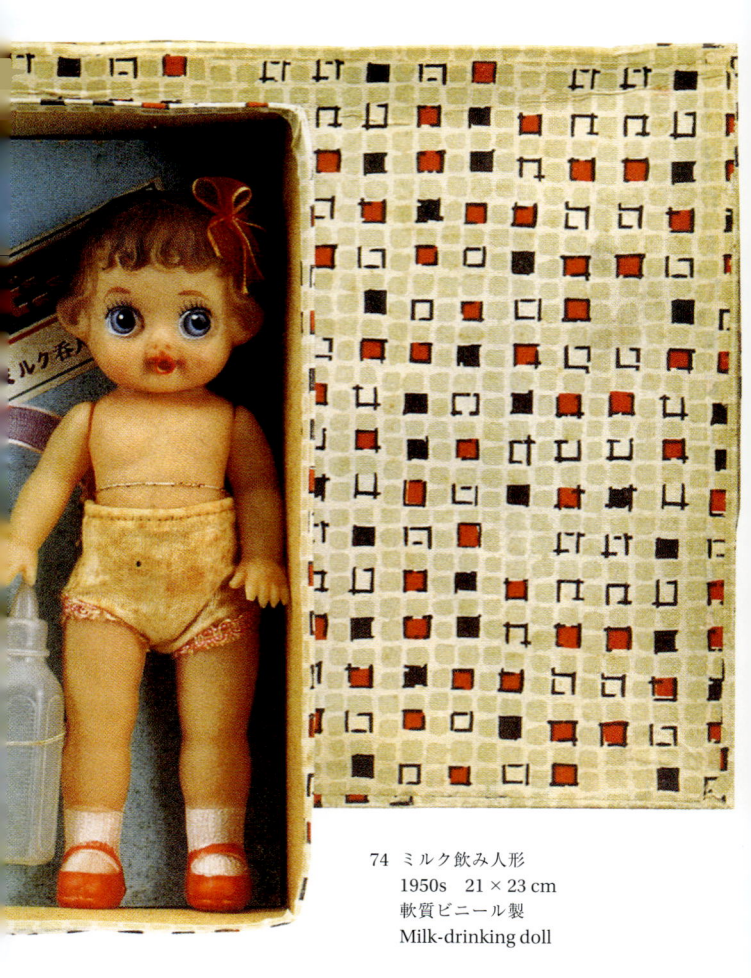

74 ミルク飲み人形
1950s　21 × 23 cm
軟質ビニール製
Milk-drinking doll

カール人形
Curl doll

75 カール人形
1950s 21 × 15 cm
軟質ビニール製
Curl doll

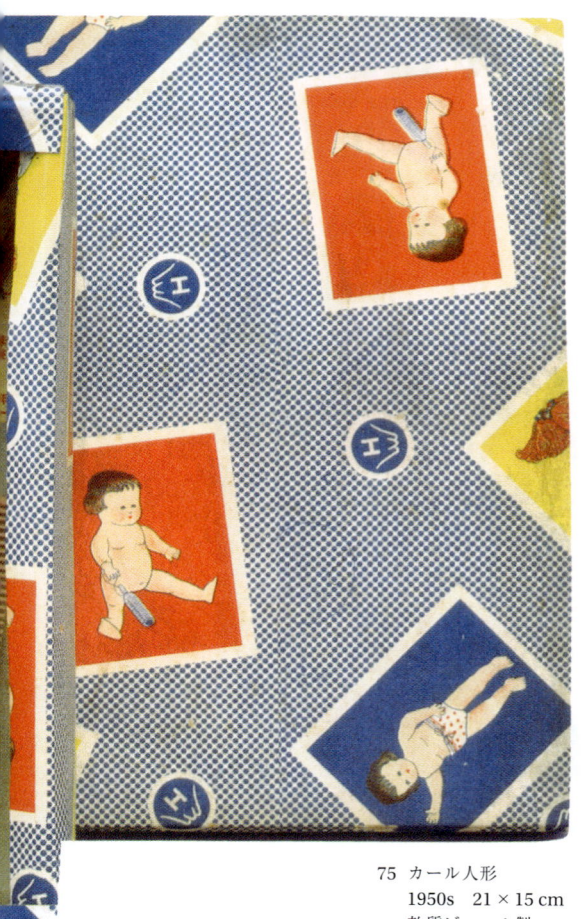

76 スキッパー人形
1960s　23.5 × 6 cm
ソフトビニール製
マテル社
Skipper

Barbie and Skipper

Barbie was first introduced to Japan in 1962 and by 1964 had become a great hit with older elementary school girls. With roughly 100 differnt outfits, changeable wigs, and characters like Barbie's little sister Skipper and boyfriend Ken, the dolls allowed for complex play. Plates No. 90-95 show original drawings, paper patterns and samples of early Barbie fashions, all considered extremely valuable.

バービー人形
Barbie

77 バービー人形
1960s　30 × 6.5 cm
ソフトビニール製
マテル社
Barbie

ウエディングドレス・デザイン原画　30 × 41.5 cm
Original drawing of a wedding dress

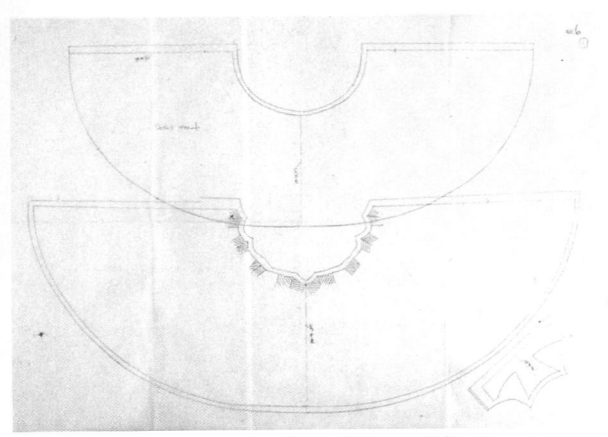

ウエディングドレスの型紙　Paper patterns

ウエディングドレス一式　A wedding dress set

バービー人形にサンプルのウエディングドレスを着せたところ
Berbie in the wedding dress

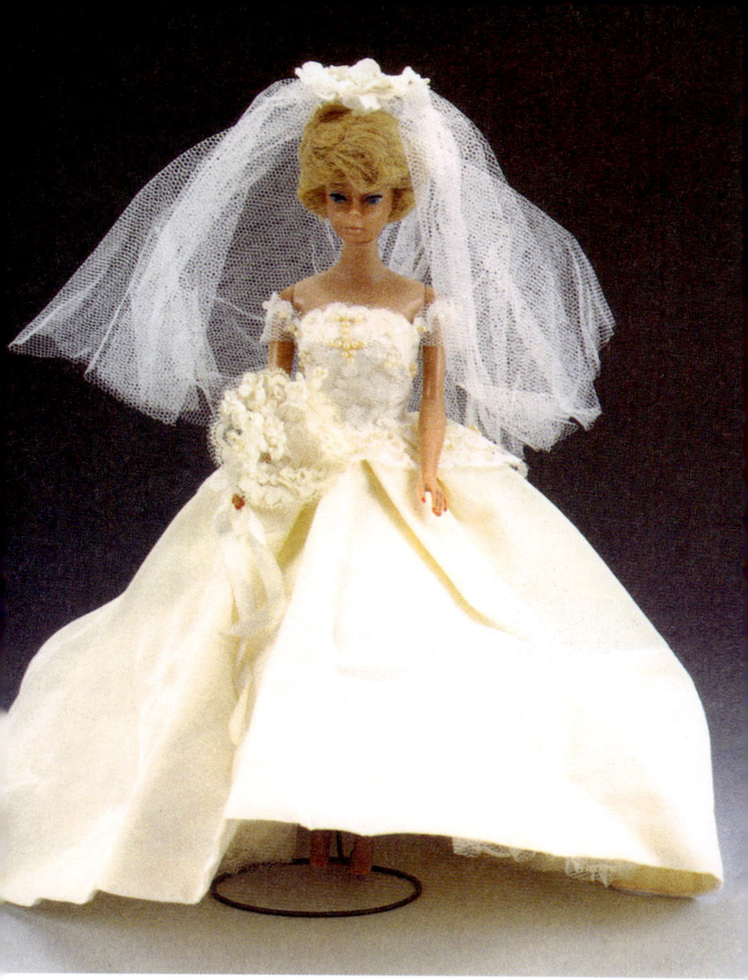

バービー・バッグ
1961年　31 × 27 × 6.5 cm
マテル社
Berbie's bag

ウエディングドレスを着たバービー
Side view of Barbie
in the wedding dress

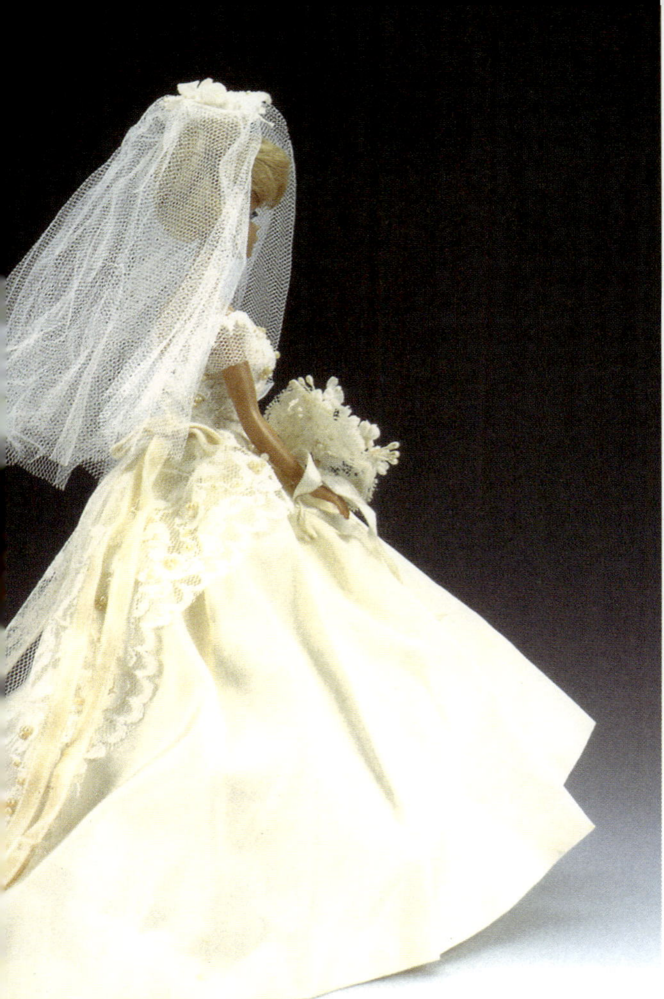

78　パットちゃん　はるみちゃん　リカちゃん　（左より）
1960s　22.5 × 4.5 cm　ソフトビニール製
Pat-chan, Harumi-chan & Rika-chan (from left to right)

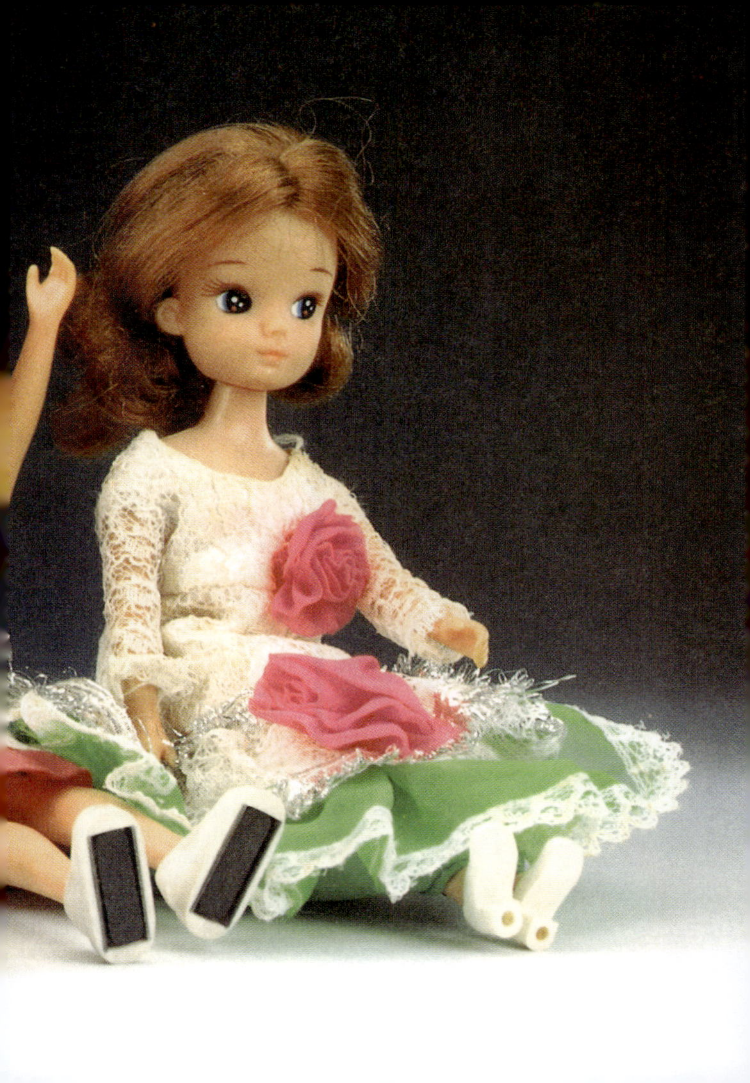

79 ジェニー
1980s　33 × 14 × 5 cm
ソフトビニール製　タカラ
Jenny

Rika-chan doll

"Rika kayama, 5th grader at Shirakaba school, birthday May 3, Taurus, O blood-type. Excels in mucic and gym, weak point arithemetic" (from *Rika-chan and Rika-chan's House*. Soichi Masubuchi). First introduced in 1967, Rica-chan, the 11-year old daughter of French musician and a Japanese designer, was the first truly Japanese fashion doll. With black hair and other common Japanese characteristics, she won immediate popularity with young girls, who could relate to her better than the previously popular Western-style dolls.

GIジョー
GI Joe

80 GIジョー
　1960s　29.5 × 13 cm
　ソフトビニール製
　HASBRO
　GI Joe

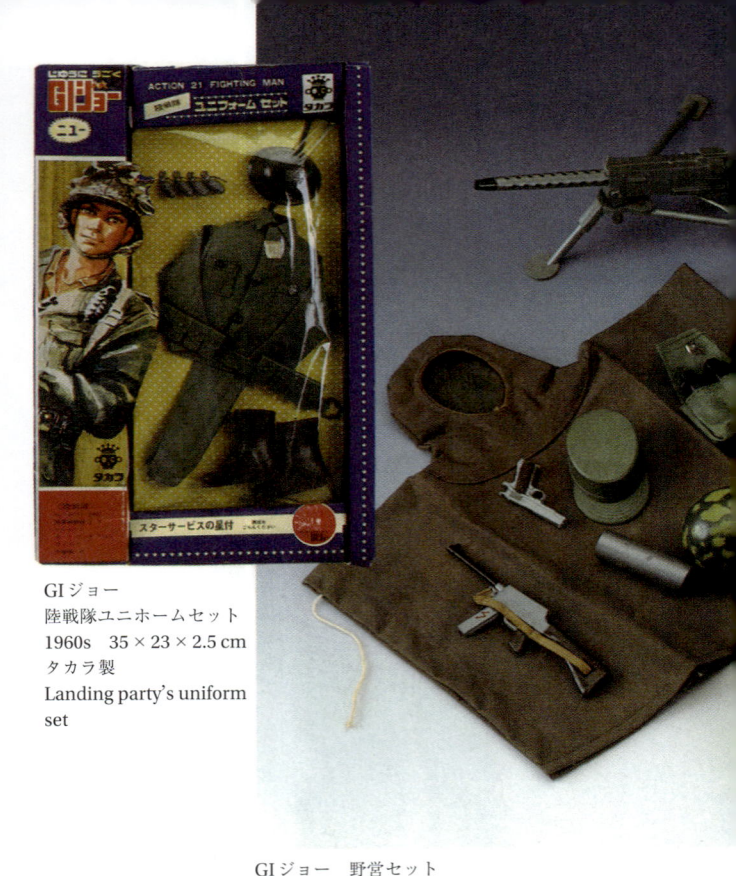

GI ジョー
陸戦隊ユニホームセット
1960s　35 × 23 × 2.5 cm
タカラ製
Landing party's uniform set

GI ジョー　野営セット
1960s　33.5 × 13.5 cm
HASBRO・タカラ製
Camping set

GI Joe

A hit in America, GI Joe was first sold in Japan in 1966 and was a favorite of Japanese boys, An American soldier, GI Joe, had 26 movable joints allowing for realistic movement. and costumes were available for the army, navy and air force of Britain, France, Germany and other nations in addiction to America. Weapons and accessories were also numerous, allowing for a great variety of combinations.

やじろべえ　*Yajirobei*

81　やじろべえの図　天明4年（1784）刊　22.5 × 16 cm
　　身をかろくこころすなをにもつ人は あぶなそうでも あぶなげもなし
　　『やしない草』　下河辺拾水画　脇坂義堂著
　　Illustration of *yajirobei* (balancing toy)

82 童児　加茂人形　江戸時代　10 × 5 cm
Yajirobei (balancing toy) made from Kamo doll of a boy's figure
バランスをとる棒の両端にガラス玉の重りがついている。

83 布袋
明治時代　2.7 × 29.5 × 1.2 cm
Yajirobei of Hotei god
京都の清水、五条坂あたりで焼かれたのであろう
石焼の布袋を買って、手と足の棒は自分で作る。

84 兵隊 ▶
1900s　16 × 14.5 cm
Yajirobei of soldier

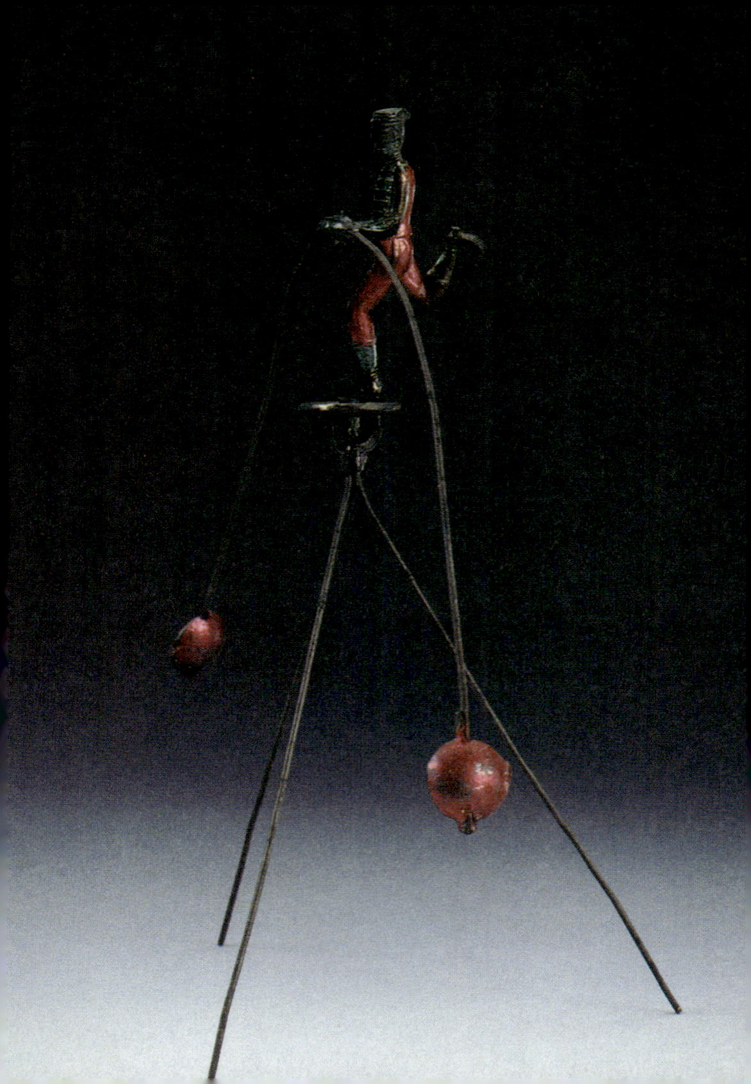

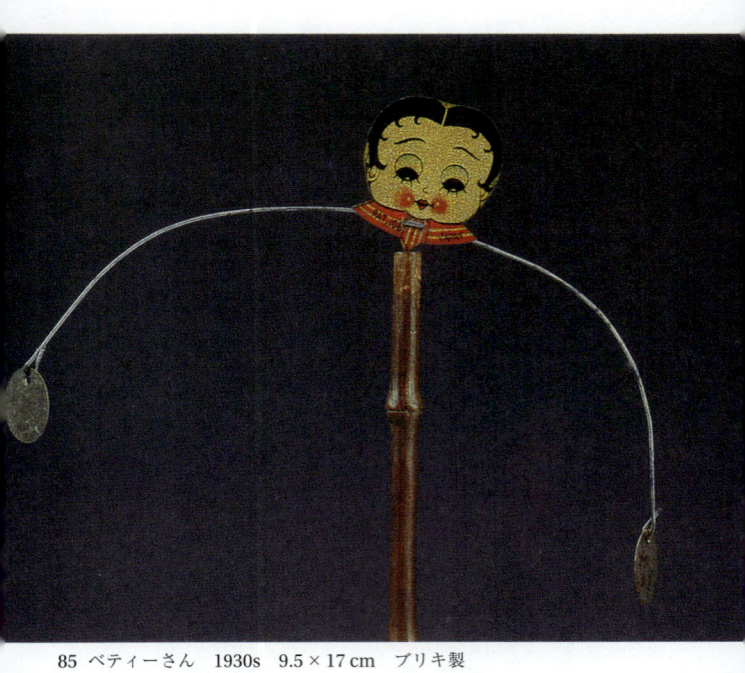

85 ベティーさん　1930s　9.5 × 17 cm　ブリキ製
Yajirobei of Betty Boop

86 とり 1950s 11.5 × 18.5 cm ブリキ製 *Yajirobei* of bird

87 犬 1950s 10 × 18.5 cm ブリキ製 *Yajirobei* of dog

うつし絵　Transfer seals

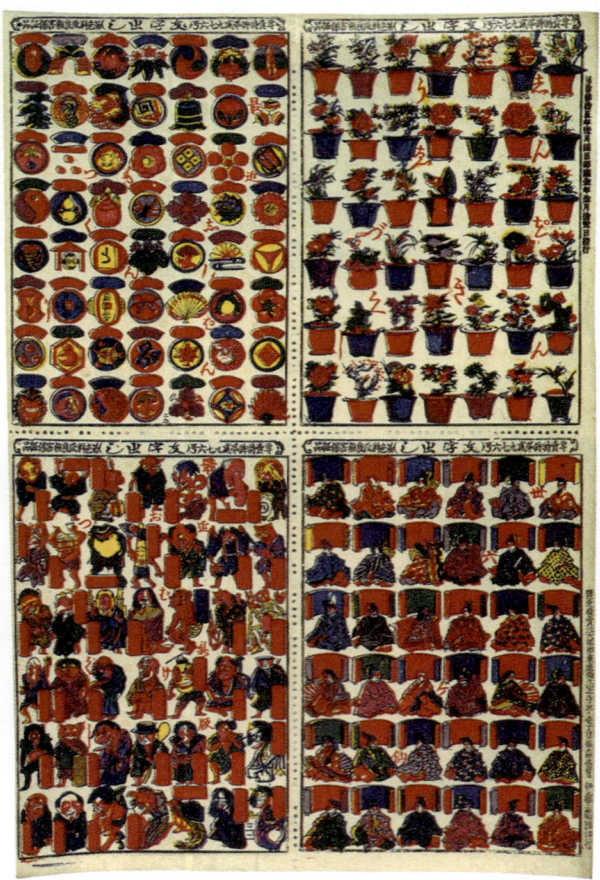

88　文字出し　明治35年（1902）　37 × 25 cm　伊藤二龍館印行
Letters & labels

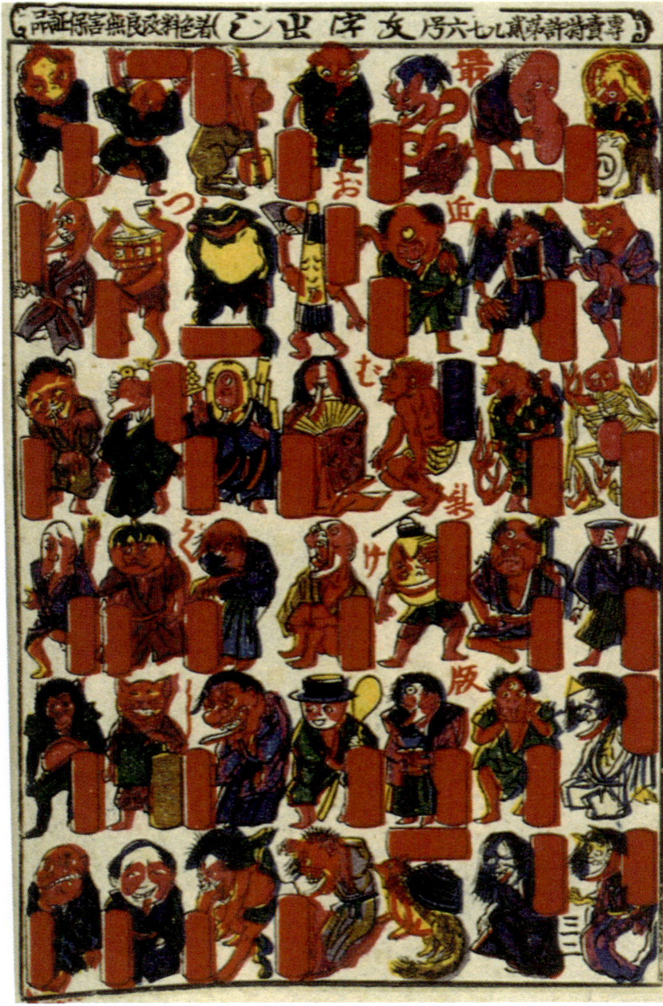
専賣特許第貳九七六号
文字出し
（著色料改良無害保証品）
最近製版

89　文字出し　明治36年（1903）　37 × 25 cm　伊藤二龍館印行
Letters & labels

專賣特許第九萬六千七百五十番 字出し 著色料改良無際繪新品

90 文字出し 明治35年（1902） 19 × 24.5 cm 伊藤二龍館印行
Letters & labels

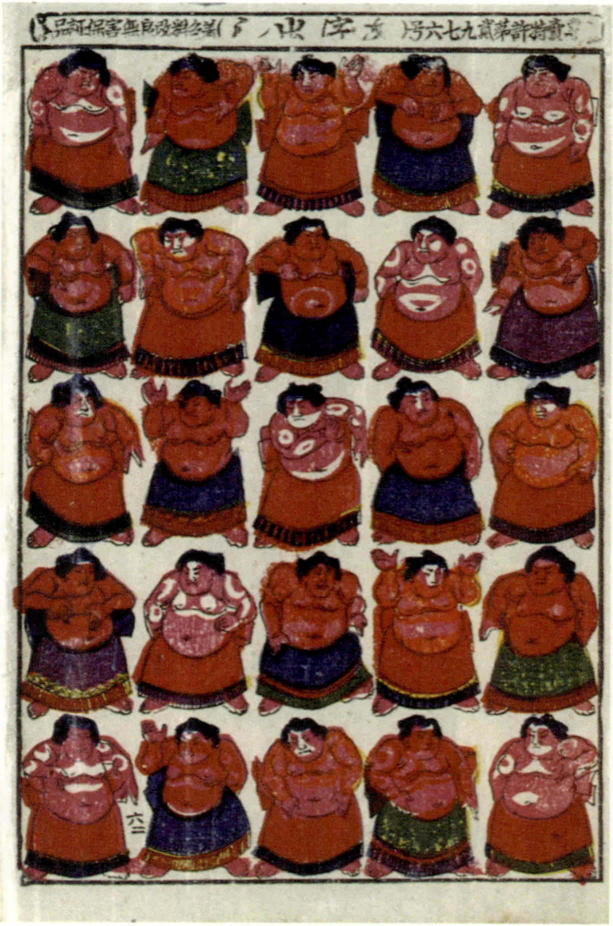
六二

91　ウツシ絵　18.5 × 25 cm　萬歳印　Letters & labels

標商（萬歲印）錄登

92　松竹少女歌劇ウツシ繪　10.5 × 21.7 cm
"Shochiku Girls' Opera"

93 　どうぶつうつしえ　昭和16年（1941）頃　21.5 × 5 × 10.7 cm　"Animal seals"

94 愛馬進軍・ウツシヱ
昭和16年（1941）　22 × 11 cm　原色版印刷社出版部発行
"My favorite horse marching"

くちを出しながら幾月か
共に死の丘でこの馬と
攻めて渡たんだ山や川
飢つた千恵氏島が立ふ

祀蔥毀のお守りを
掛けて戦ふこの栗毛
ちりにまみれた鬣街に
なんでなつくく顔よせて

伊達には取らぬこの銃
とつきかかけて突込めば
なんともういぞ敵の陣馬よ磨け悲閾犬

お前の骨の上の上に
立て入城の凱歌
兵に努らぬ天晴の
動は永く忘れぬぞ

毎日話したトーチカや
今日は貢壁の鳥居
馬もくっすり腰られるよ
從いても柱を良はしたぞ

彈丸の雨緑る髭散
封緒むように乗り切つて
ってもたしたあの時
明日の戦は手輕いぞ

95 　兵隊さんありがたう・ウツシヱ
　　昭和16年（1941）　12×10.4 cm　松本かつぢ作・原色版印刷社出版部発行
　　"Thank you soldiers"

寺特賣 第一一張 五大國圖 (時局版)

干特賣 第一一張 五大國圖 (防諜版)

96 少國民ウツシヱ・四季の花
　　25 × 12.5 cm　ホシ玩具出版社発行
　　"Seasonal flowers"

159

97　慰問用うつし絵とシール
　　昭和17年（1942）　23×8.8 cm　中原淳一絵　キヨト社発行
　　"Lovely lady seals"

161

98 　文化ウツシエ・皇軍御慰問
　　昭和17年（1942）　20 × 10 cm　大森商店発行
　　"Comforts for Imperial Army"

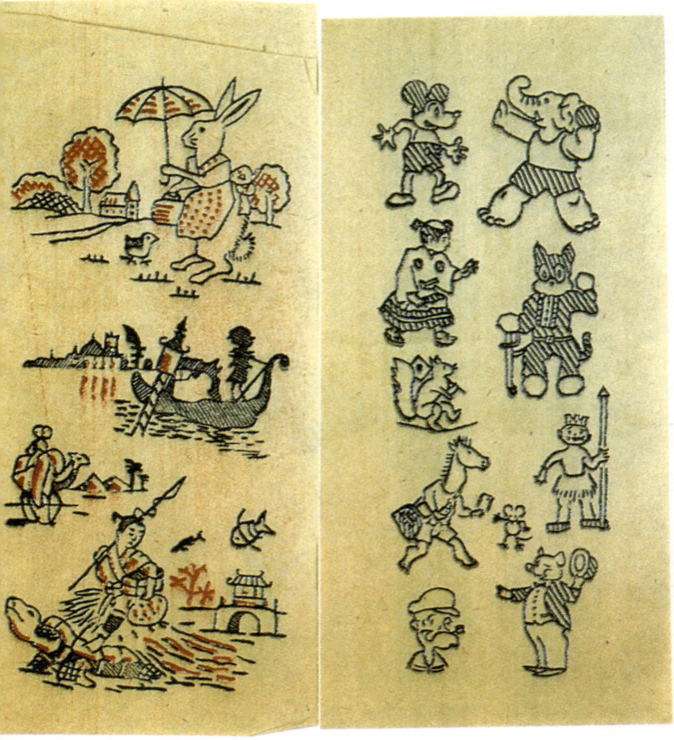

99 うつしえ 19.3 × 8.7 cm Letters & labels

うつしえ

A エー	B ピー	C シー
D ディー	E イー	F エフ
G ジー	H エッチ	I アイ
J ジェー	K ケー	L エル
	M エム	

うつしえ

N エヌ	O オー	P ピー
Q キュー	R アール	S エス
T ティー	U ユー	V ヴイ
W ダブリュー	X エックス	Y ワイ
	Z ゼット	SAAKASU

100 うつしえ 19 × 13.5 cm "Hero seals"

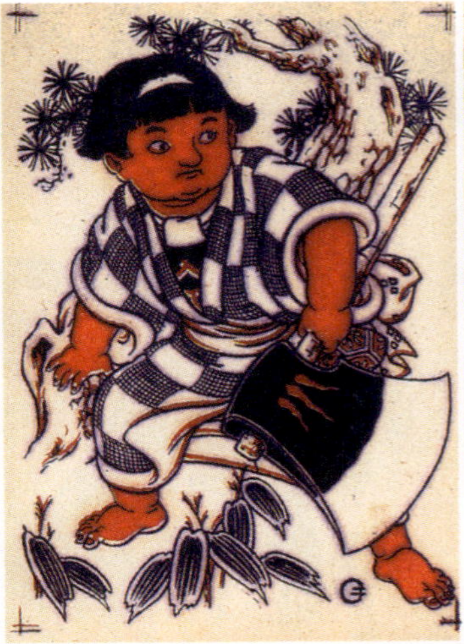

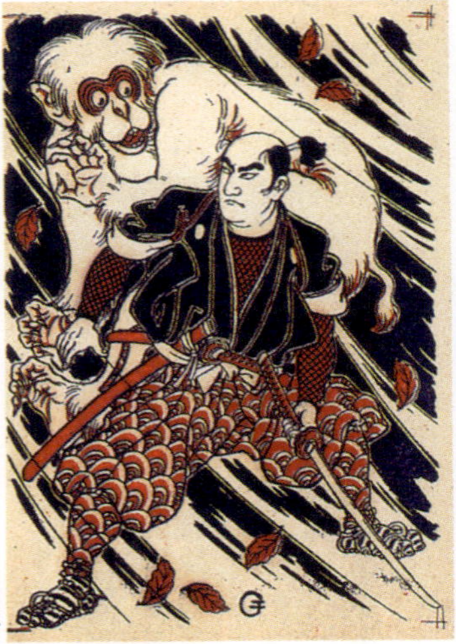

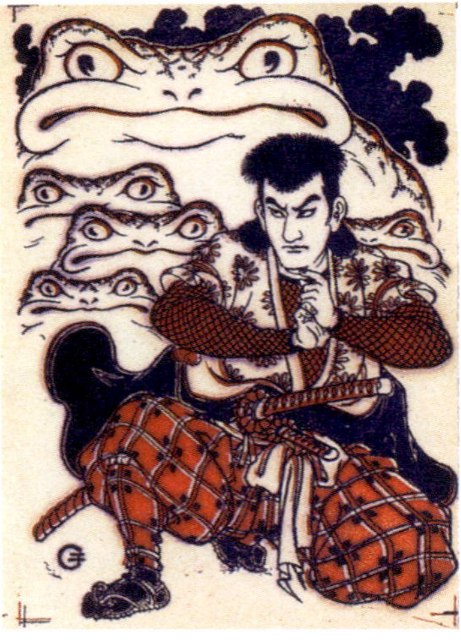

101 すみれうつしえ
18 × 7.6 cm／20 × 7.3 cm
日光社発行
Transfer Pictures "Baseball players"

102　腕章　サンフランシスコ・シールズ
　　　日米親善野球試合・切符
　　　昭和24年（1949）　9.7×16 cm／4.7×10cm
　　　"San Francisco seals": arm band & ticket

103 うつしえ　15×6cm　ニコニコ社　ナゴヤ玩具
   "Amusing seals"

171

104 最新版　速寫早うつしえ　26 × 18.5 cm　"Children seals"

最新版 速寫 早うつしえ

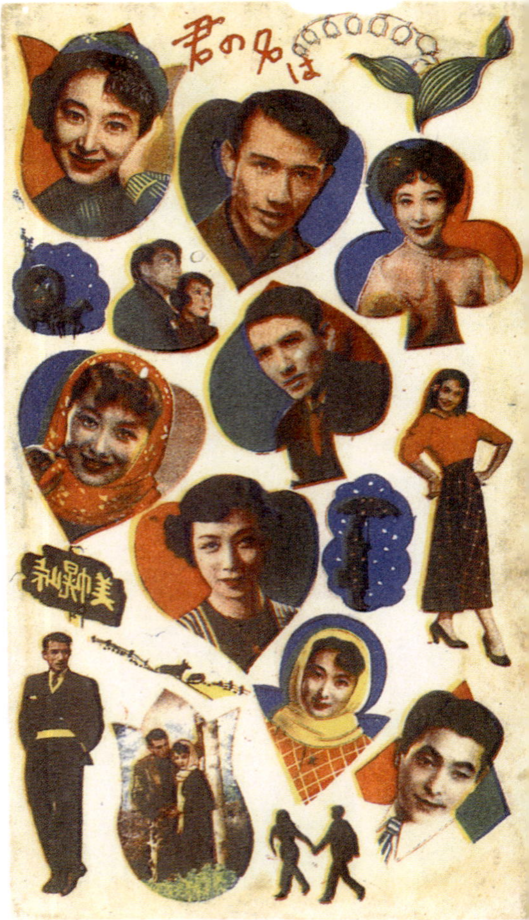
君の名は

105
君の名は　うつしえ
昭和27年（1952）
20 × 11 cm
Transfer seals with characters from the story "Your name?"

106 アトムうつしえ
21 × 11.5 cm
カゴメ玩具
"Stars of stage and screen"

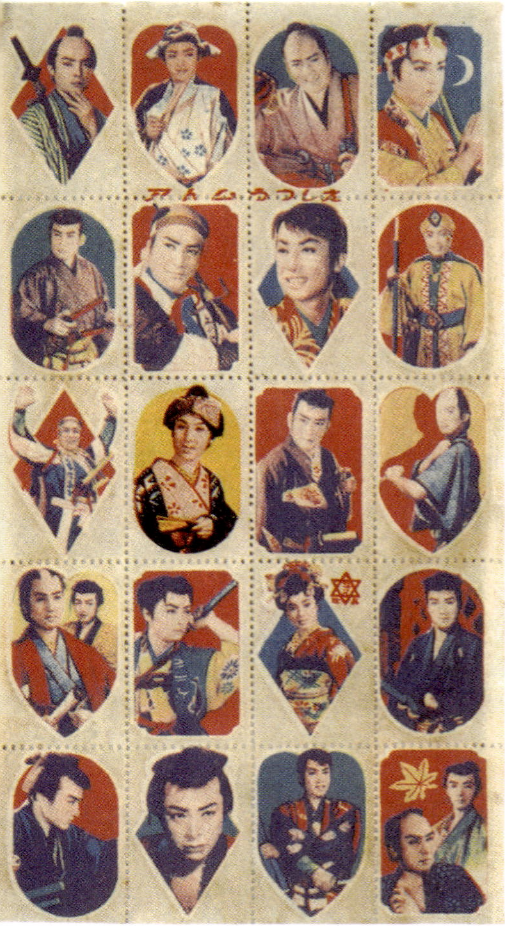
アトムうつしえ

107 うつし絵
20.5 × 10.5 cm
"Superheroes"

179

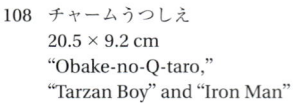

108 チャームうつしえ
20.5 × 9.2 cm
"Obake-no-Q-taro,"
"Tarzan Boy" and "Iron Man"

チャームうつしえ

着せかえ Dress-up paper dolls

109　西洋着せ替　36 × 25.5 cm　文部省製本所発行　"Western dresses"

110 キセカエ 36 × 24 cm "Western dresses"

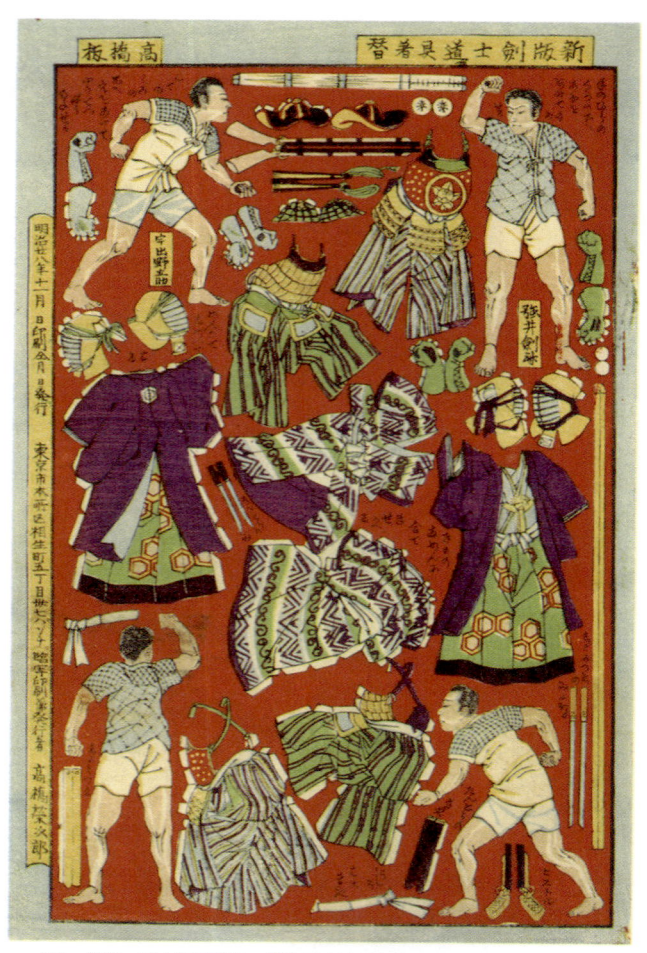

111　新版　剣士道具着替　明治28年（1895）　37 × 24.7 cm
高橋版　"Fencing equipment"

112 志ん板　阿称様起せかゑ　明治27年（1894）　37 × 25 cm
よし藤画　越米版　"*Anesana* dolls"

113 おどりのいせう付　明治29年（1896）　37.5×25 cm　越米版
"Dancing costumes"

114　志ん板　いせうつけ　明治30年（1897）　37 × 25 cm　越米画版
松野栄次郎発行　"Men's formal wear"

115　ねいさんのきせかえ　明治31年（1898）　37×25 cm　越米版
"My elder sister's dresses"

116　おどりいせうつけ　明治32年（1899）　38 × 25 cm　越米版
"Dancing costumes"

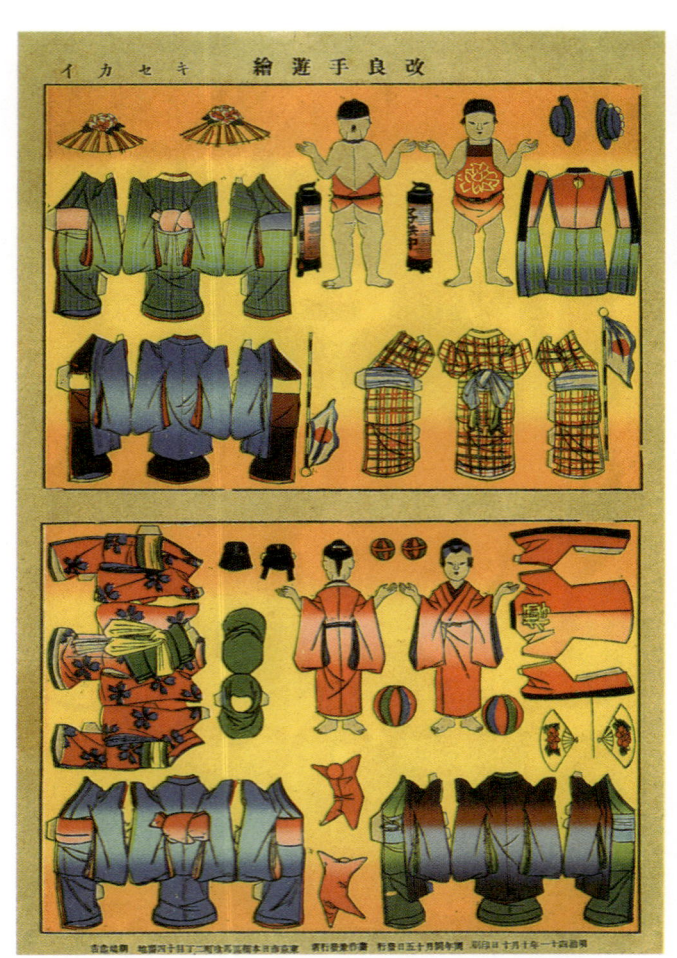

117　改良手遊繪・キセカイ　明治41年（1908）　37.5 × 25 cm　綱島亀吉発行
"Boys' and girls' festive kimonos"

118 新版キセカエ 41 × 29.5 cm "New family fashions"

192

120　キセカヘ・フランス人形　26 × 20 × 2.5 cm　YOSHIO　"French dolls"

◀ 119　新版キセカエ
　　41 × 29 cm
　　"New family fashions"

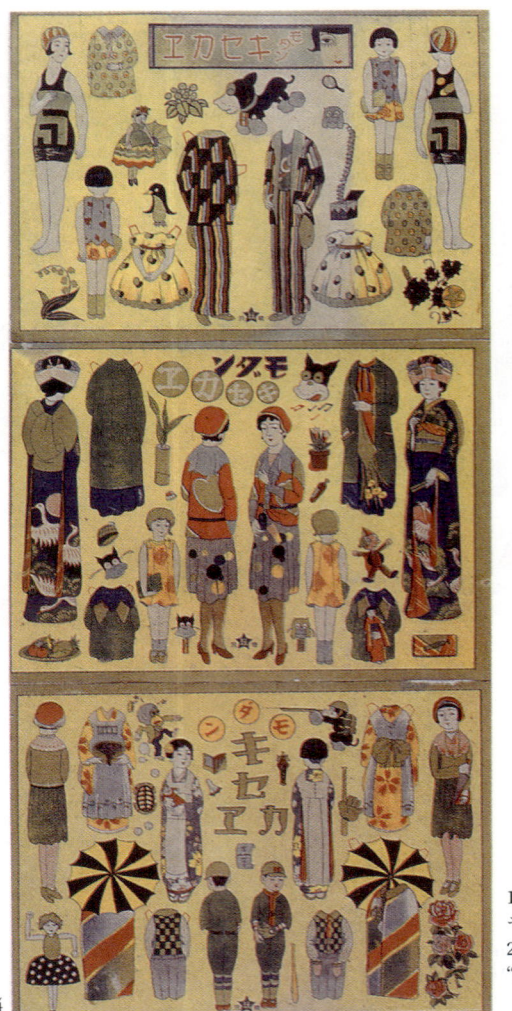

121
モダンキセカエ
20 × 27.5 cm
"Modern fashions"

122　仲ヨシ・キセカエ人形　26.5 × 20 × 2 cm　国民航空教材株式会社
"Friends"

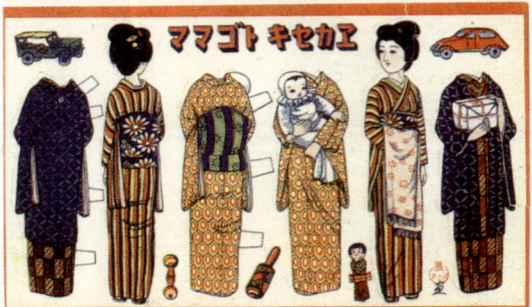

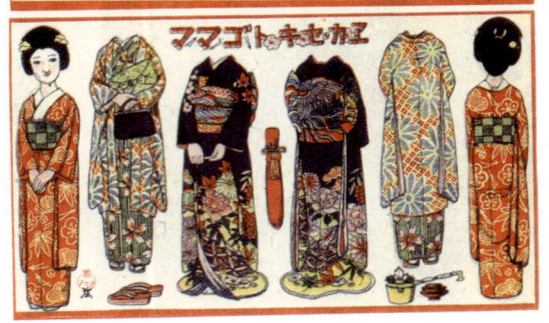

123　ママゴトキセカエ　15.5 × 26 cm　"Playing house"

124　きせがえ　15.3 × 10.5 cm　"Fashions"（front & back figures）

125　マンガきせがえ　17.6 × 13 cm　ライオン玩具　"Comic characters"

126
でこちゃんの
きせかえ
26.5 × 19 cm
"Deko-chan"

127
きせかえ
25.7 × 25 cm
"Mother and daughter fashions"

128
はるひこのきせかえ
38 × 17.5 cm
東京不二紙工製
"Haruhiko's dress-up paper dolls"

129　最新版キセカエアソビ　38.5 × 31.5 × 17.8 cm
"New woman's fashions"

130　スワンきせかえ　23 × 15.5 cm　"Mother and child fashions"

131　朝日のきせかえ　26 × 18 cm　"Takarazuka costumes"

203

132 朝日のきせかえ 26 × 18 cm "Takarazuka costumes"

133　君の名は　きせかえ　昭和27年（1952）　26 × 20 cm
Haruki's fashion (hero of the story "Your name?")

134　ロマンきせかえ　30.5 × 21 cm　"Romantic fashions"

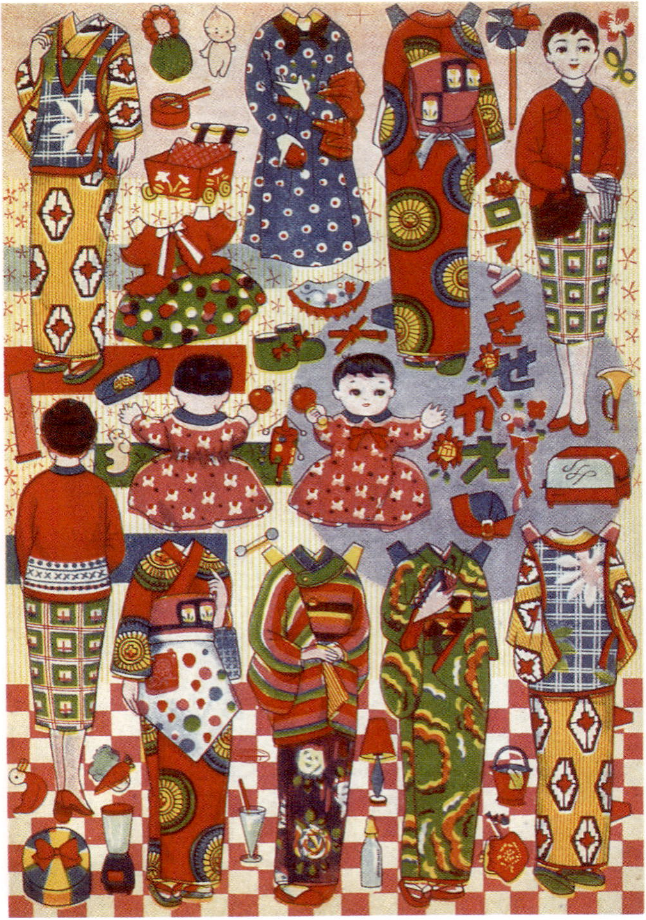
ロマンきせかえ

135 花嫁きせかえ 昭和34年（1959） 30.5 × 21 cm
Wedding of Crown Prince and Princess

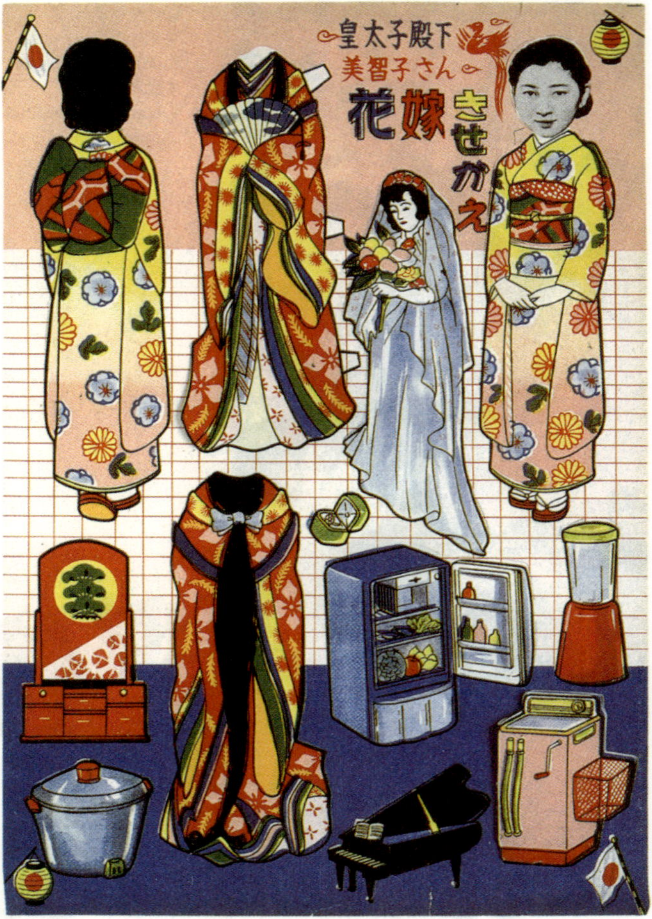
皇太子殿下
美智子さん
花嫁きせかえ

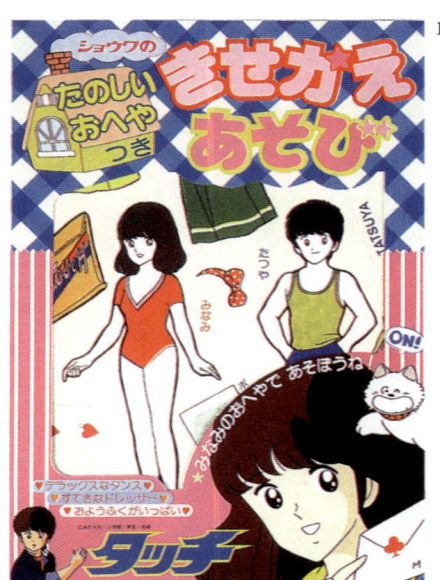

136 きせかえあそび
30.5 × 21.5 cm
©あだち充／小学館
東宝　旭通
Dress-up paper dolls with comic story "Touch"

ぬり絵　Coloring books (Nuri-e)

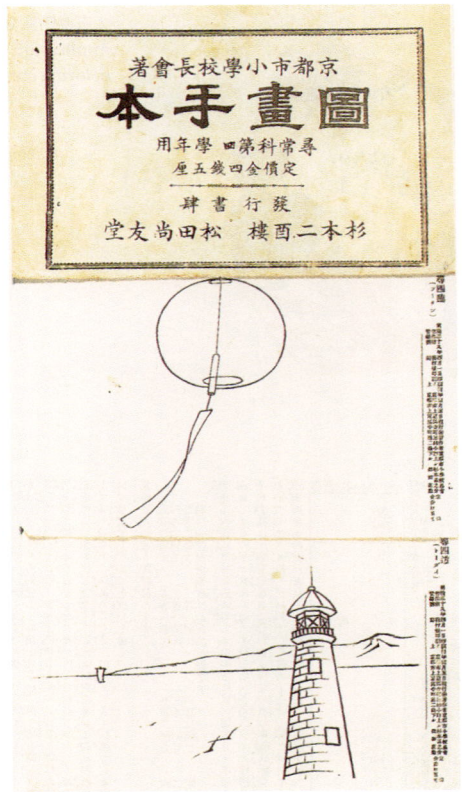

137　図画手本
　　　明治38年（1905）　15 × 23 cm
　　京都市小学校校長会著　松田尚友堂発行
　　"Coloring book for elementary school students"

138 教育彩画紙
明治38年（1905）
15.3 × 19.5 cm
大阪奨励館発行
Application form for coloring contest

139　日本少年第18回懸賞彩色絵端書　14.2 × 9.2 cm
Postcard to be colored for coloring contest

140 ぬり絵カード
5.3 × 8.5 cm
Pencil sketches for coloring

214

141 サイシキシカタ・エンピツ画（ぬりえ帳）　大正7年（1918）　22 × 15.5 cm
綱島亀吉発行　"A boy and his dog"

142　ぬり絵　22 × 30 cm　"Zoo coloring book"

KUMA
熊
クマ

143　ヌリエ
　　昭和11年（1936）　19.5 × 31.5 × 2 cm
　　株式会社春江堂発行
　　"Designs for a happy child"

144　コドモヌリヱ　13.7 × 26 × 2 cm　"Enjoy coloring"

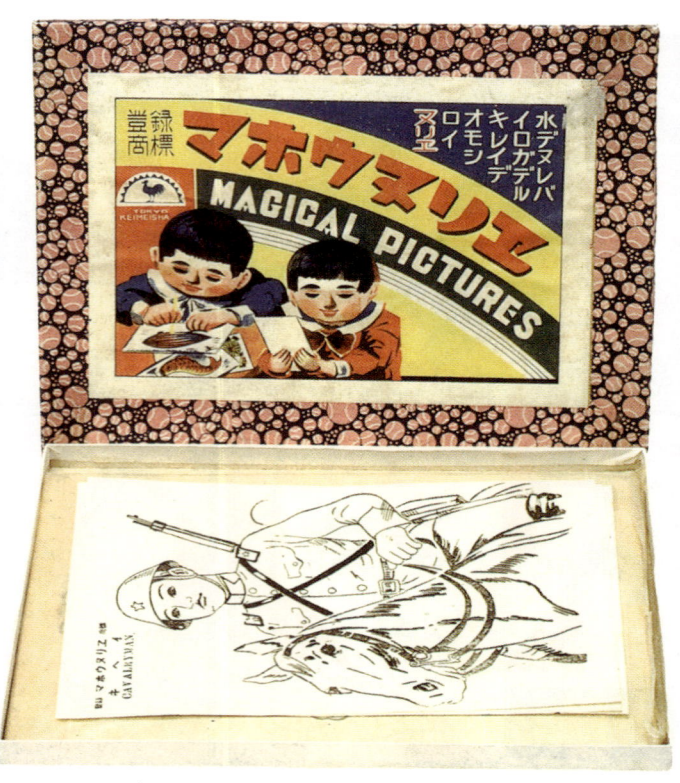

145 マホウヌリエ
17.5 × 24 × 1.5 cm
TOKYO KEIMEISHA
"Magical pictures"

146 ヨイコヌリヱ
  15 × 21 cm
  "Wartime companion for good children"

147
ヨイコヌリエ
15 × 21 cm
"Wartime companion for good children"

148
ヨイコヌリヱ
15 × 21 cm
"Wartime companion for good children"

149　連続ヌリエ・鐘の鳴る丘　昭和22年（1947）　13.3×11 cm　たまよ画
"Story coloring book"

150 ぬり絵 25 × 18.3 cm "Playtime"

151 新版ぬりえ
25 × 18.3 cm
"Coloring book for girls"

152　ひろしのぬりゑ　16×12 cm　東京児童工作社発行
"Hiroshi's coloring books"

153　きれいなぬりえ　昭和24年(1949)　18×13 cm　本田のり子画
日照館書店発行　"coloring book for girls"

227

154　ぬりえ　昭和26年（1951）　26×18.5 cm　梅原龍三郎・安井曾太郎編集指導
　　暮しの手帖社発行　"Coloring practice"

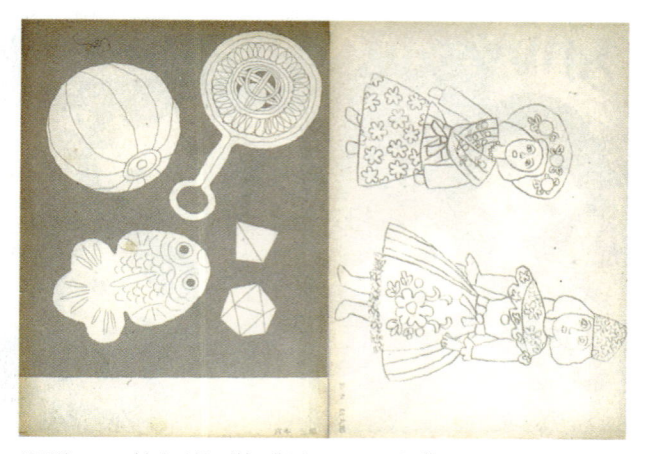

練習帖の一つ（宮本三郎・絵）　"Coloring practice"

155 ぬりえ
21.5 × 15.5 cm
"Comic series"

156 変身ぬりえ
21.5 × 15.5 cm
"Mutant series"

157　ぬりえ
21.5 × 31 cm
"Comic series"

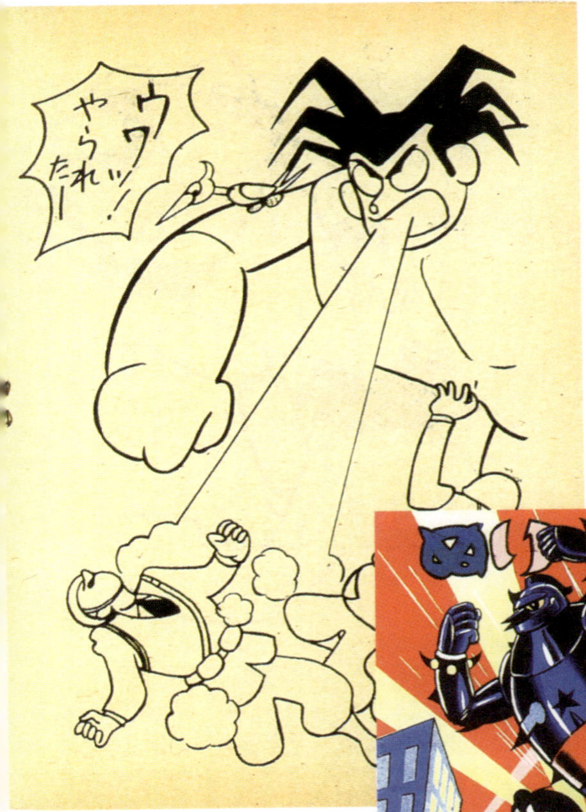
ウワッ！
やられたー

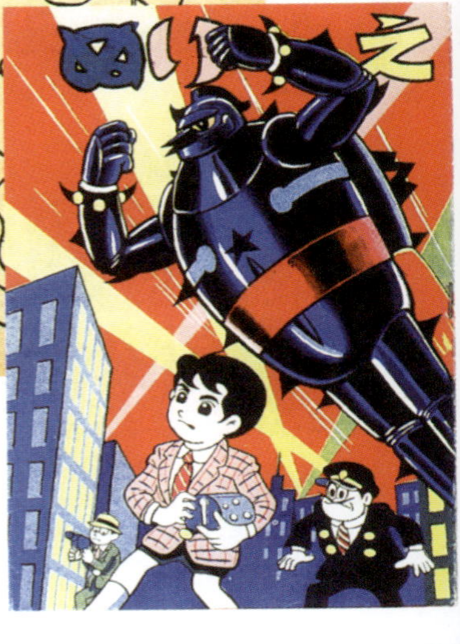

きいちのぬりえ Kiichi's Coloring Books

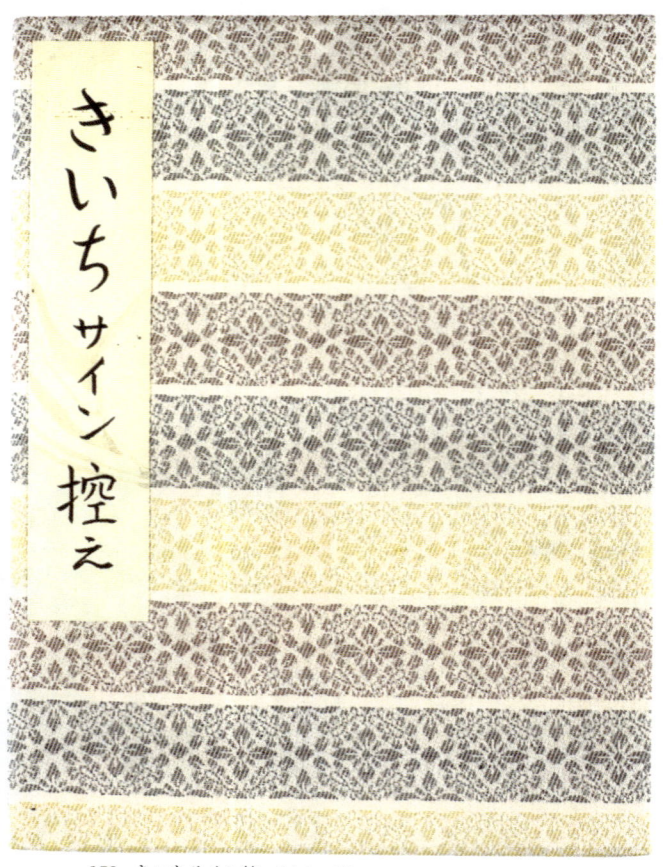

158　きいちサイン控　24.4 × 18 cm

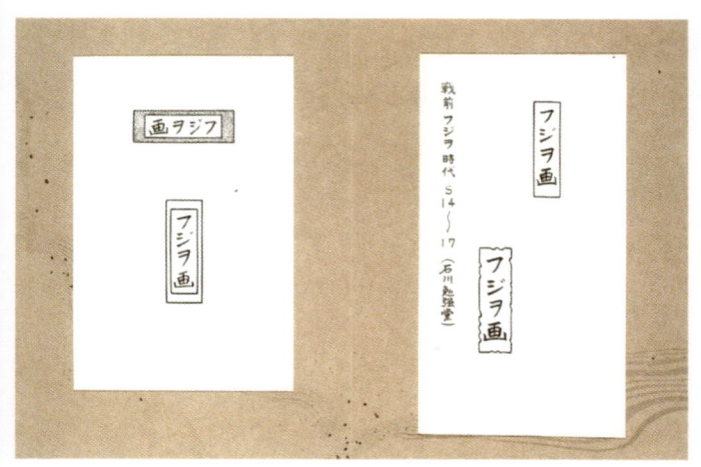

159　フジヲ時代　昭和14〜17年　石川勉強堂

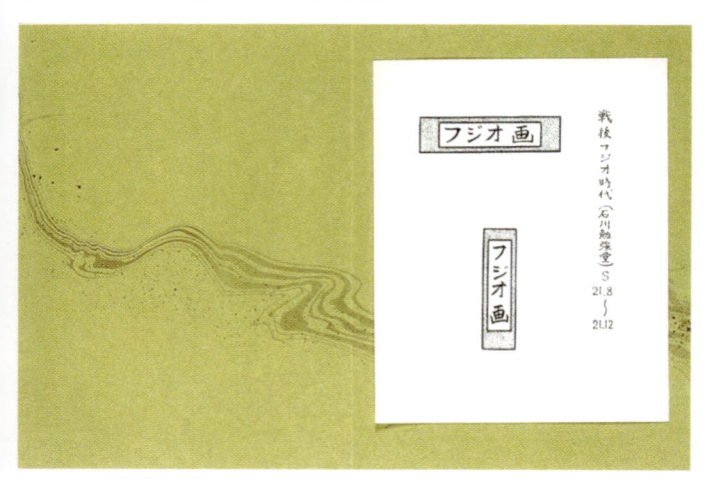

160　フジオ時代　昭和21年　石川勉強堂

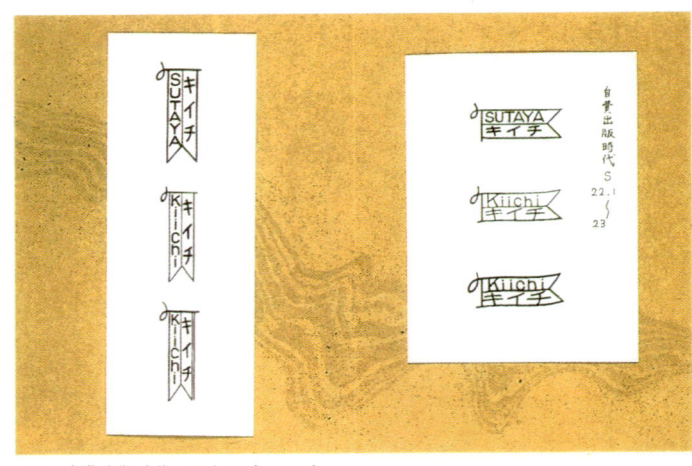

161　自費出版時代　昭和22年・23年

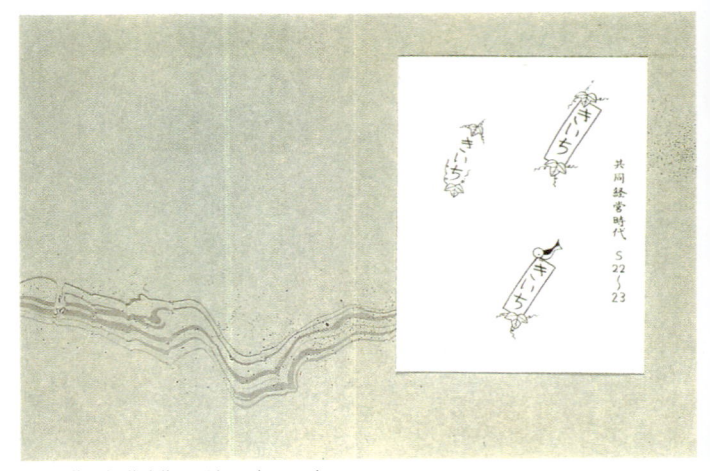

162　共同経営時代　昭和22年・23年

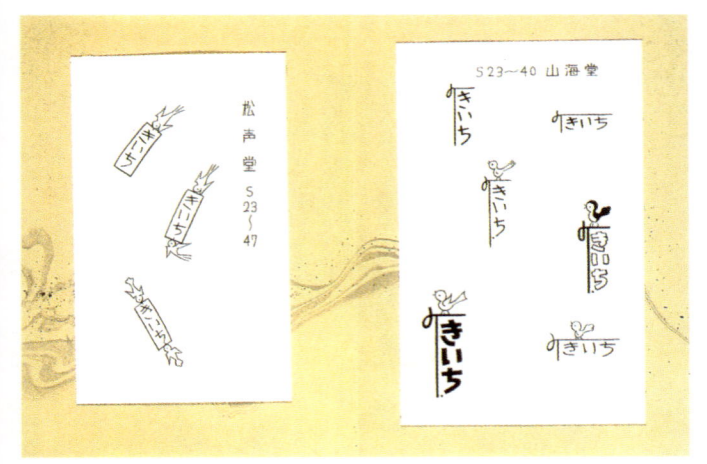

163　昭和23～40年（右）　山海堂　昭和23～47年（左）　松声堂

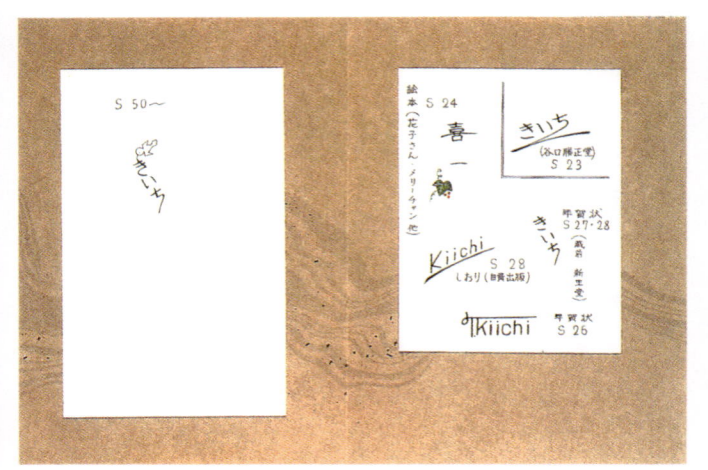

164　昭和23～28年（右）　昭和50年～（左）

235

165 フジヲ時代　昭和14〜17年

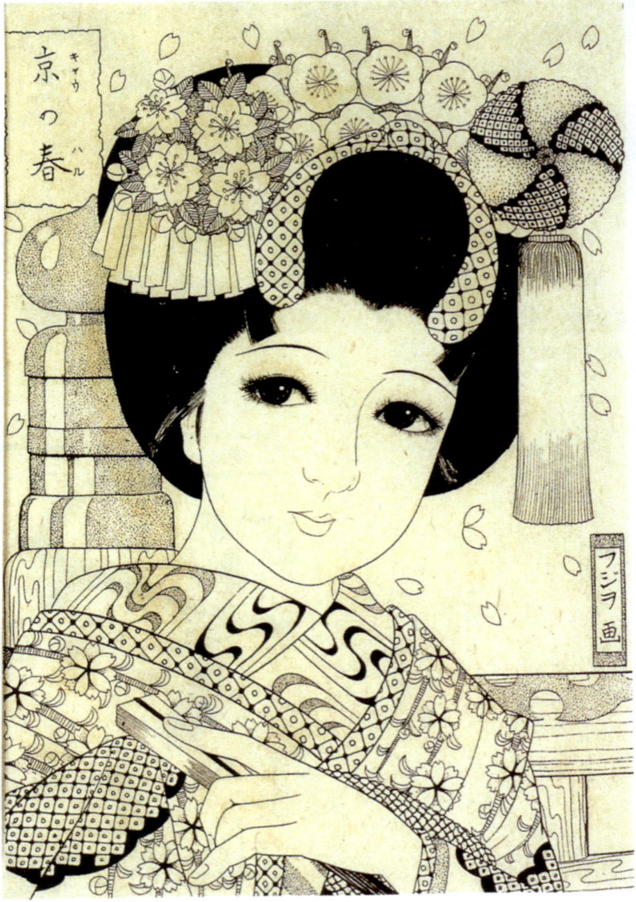
京の春
フジヲ画

166 昭和22〜23年

167 フジヲ時代
　　昭和14〜17年

239

168 ぬりゑ
昭和23〜24年
石川聲堂

169　ぬりゑ
　　　昭和23〜24年

170 蔦谷氏に「メリーちゃん」の表紙絵を肉筆で再現してもらったもの。

171 メリーちゃん▶
25.5 × 35.5 cm
画・蔦谷喜一　文・美保優
朝日出版社

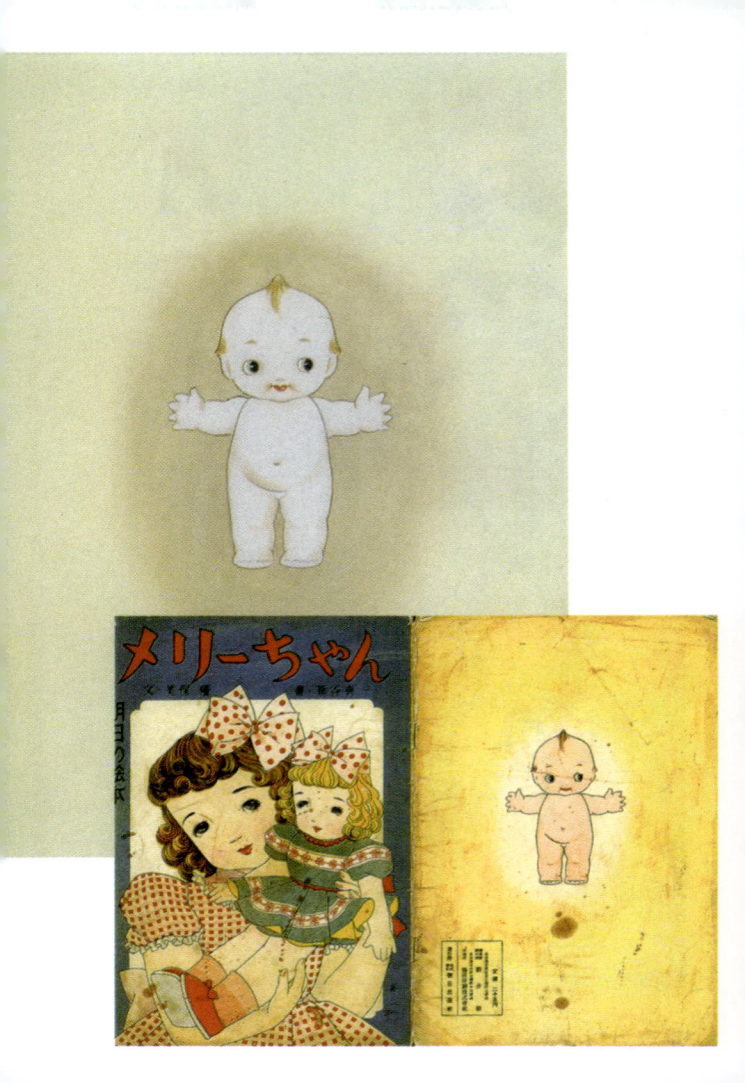

メリーちゃん

172 はなこさん 昭和24年

はなこさん

173 ぬりえ 昭和20年代 石川松聲堂

174 ぬりえ　昭和30年代　川村山海堂

175 ぬりえ 昭和30年代 石川松聲堂

176 ぬりえ 昭和30年代 石川松聲堂

177　きいちのきせかえ　昭和30年代

178　きせかえ　昭和30年代

179　きせかえの表紙の原画　昭和35年頃

180　ぬりえ　昭和35年頃

181　おあそびぬりえ　昭和40年代

182　おとぎばなしぬりえ　昭和40年代

183 ぬりえ原画　昭和50年代

184 ぬりえ原画 昭和50年代

人形 Dolls
紫紅社文庫

2015年(平成27年)6月28日　第1刷発行

著　者	多田敏捷
編　集	濱田信義
写　真	亀村俊二
発行者	勝丸裕哉
発行所	紫紅社

〒605-0089
京都市東山区古門前通大和大路東入ル元町367
電　話　075-541-0206
ＦＡＸ　075-541-0209
http://www.artbooks-shikosha.com/

印刷製本　　日新印刷株式会社

©Toshikatsu Tada, Shikosha 2015　Printed in Japan
ISBN978-4-87940-615-6 C0172
定価はカバーに表示してあります。